HANNA-BARBERA'S

SCOOBY-DO

ANNUAL

CONTENTS

The Vampire Valley Mystery 5
Dead Ends! 11
Knock, Knock 12
Night for a Fright (part 1) 13
Scooby's Crossword 21
Spangles, Sawdust . . . and Scooby Doo! 22
Night for a Fright (part 2) 27
Escape from the Spook! 36
A Monster Collage 38
Ghostly Guffaws 39
Happy Birthday, Scooby Doo! 40
Send a Secret Message 46
Night for a Fright (part 3) 48
Ghostly Giggles! 56
Scooby Doo, Phantom Hound 57

Published in Great Britain by
World International Publishing Limited.
A Pentos Company,
P.O. Box 111, Great Ducie Street, Manchester M60 3BL.
Printed in Italy.
SBN 7235 6688 7.

The Vampire Valley Mystery

Night was falling as the Mystery Machine drove slowly along a deserted highway in the cactus-filled desert known as Vampire Valley, way out west. Here the gang had been spending a few days away from it all. The trouble was they had been spending rather lavishly too, and now they were tired, hungry and very, very broke!

"I don't think we'll ever taste food again," groaned Shaggy, as he absently chewed on the end of an empty bag of popcorn. "I wonder how cooked cactus tastes?"

"Scooby oooh!" muttered Scooby, opening one eye, and trying not to listen too hard. Cactus was prickly . . . *he* knew that . . . and no money for food meant no money for bones! That just didn't bear thinking about!

"Well, you may find out shortly if things don't improve," grinned Daphne. "Hey, watch out, Freddy, you nearly ran over that guy."

"But where did he come from?" asked Freddy as he screeched to a halt. "He seems to have just appeared out of thin air!"

"Oooh ooh . . . here we go again," murmured Velma. "Ghosts seem to follow us even on vacation."

"This guy's no ghost . . . he looks as if he's just seen one!" replied Freddy. "Hi, there, is anything wrong? Can we help?"

"Only if you turn round and give me a lift out of this place," replied the man. "No wonder they offer free bed and board at that crumby castle if anyone is willing to stay the night. They know nobody will stay long enough to take up the offer. It's got the right name . . . Vampire Castle . . . and the caretakers Mr and Mrs Drack . . . a real good name for them, I guess. Gee, there's a bus . . . I'll get that . . . but if I was you guys I'd turn back now . . . while you've still got the strength to drive away . . . vampires suck blood, you know."

And with one final frightened glance backwards he ran across the highway and jumped onto the moving bus, as if terrified that the driver wouldn't stop.

"Well, that's our problem solved," said Freddy, as the bus disappeared from view. "Let's find Vampire Castle and take advantage of their kind free hospitality."

"I've suddenly stopped feeling hungry," said Velma.

"Scooby too!" added Scooby. Ghosts just weren't his scene really, but the gang never quite realised that.

"Look, Freddy, there's the castle, up there on that ridge on the right," cried Daphne. "Gee, it does look kind of creepy, but any port in a storm, I suppose."

"Or any castle in a hunger crisis," quipped Freddy, as he drove up the steep path to the castle.

Out everyone got and Daphne knocked on the door.

It was opened by a woman dressed all in black. She had grey hair scraped back from her face and cold blue eyes. She tried to give them a friendly smile, but her fang-like teeth scared Scooby so much that he cowered and jumped right into Shaggy's arms in fright.

"I suppose you're looking for shelter for the night. I'm Mrs Drack," said the woman, ushering them into the large, dark hall. "Luckily, we've plenty of rooms. You can have one each, even that dog, if you like."

"Two will be enough," said Daphne hastily. "Velma and I will share and Scooby can bunk with the boys."

"Suit yourselves . . . come this way," sniffed the woman. "Drack, help these folks with their luggage."

A small man shuffled out of the shadows, just as sinister as his wife. He leered at the gang and attempted to pat Scooby, who backed away in horror.

Drack glared at Scooby as the dog cowered behind Freddy.

"Thanks, but we can manage," Freddy said. "Just show us where we will sleep."

"And where we'll be eating," added Shaggy eagerly. "And can you bring a big bone for Scooby, please?"

"Certainly," smiled Mrs Drack. "The dining room's just over there."

"Let's eat now," cried Shaggy, rushing over quickly.

The others followed him in quickly as they heard Shaggy give a cry of dismay.

"What's wrong, Shaggy?" asked Velma. "Gee, just look at that food. It's horrible!"

And it sure was!

Everything was red . . . just like blood. Red bread, butter, rare red meat, red salad, red puddings, red jelly, red potatoes and a juicy red bone . . . just what Scooby loved!

The others watched Scooby and Shaggy tuck into the red food – Shaggy didn't care what colour the food was if it tasted good, and the red potatoes, red peas and red pies were simply delicious!

"Hey, this red cake isn't bad," said Velma trying a slice.

"Try the red juice," suggested Freddy to Daphne.

"Ugh, no, it looks just like blood," retorted Daphne. "Listen, I can hear Mrs Drack talking to someone outside."

The gang crept to the door and Freddy opened it just enough to peep outside.

Scooby gave a yell of surprise, which Shaggy quickly muffled.

"It's the guy who got on the bus," whispered Daphne. "What's *he* doing back here?"

Freddy put a finger to his lips and they all listened.

"Those kids fell for my story hook, line and sinker," said the man. "I knew they would. Now all we need to do is keep them out of the way while we stash those counterfeit notes in their van and we're away. We'll be out of the state before they're discovered."

"Right, Zake, I'll lock them in their rooms when they go upstairs," promised Mrs Drack.

"That's what you think," murmured Daphne, as she watched the bus man disappear down the winding stairs.

"Mrs Drack, could we see you for a moment?" called Freddy.

As Mrs Drack walked through the door, Freddy and Daphne seized her and bundled her into a large cupboard, and locked the door securely.

"That takes care of her," muttered Freddy. "Come on, gang, we must find those notes. Take care, the money thieves might be armed."

Scooby blanched at these words, and he and Shaggy followed the others slowly, Shaggy pausing in the hall to pick up a long pikestaff held by an old knight in armour.

But the gang must have heard their footsteps on the stairs, and as Freddy and the girls cautiously crept along a passage, the man called Zake suddenly popped out of the shadows, holding a gun.

"In here," he snarled, "and be quick about it."

Freddy and the girls found themselves in a small room where Mr Drack was busy putting dollar bills in cardboard boxes.

"Help him!" ordered Zake.

Daphne and Velma looked helplessly at Freddy, who nodded grimly.

Meanwhile Shaggy, armed with his pikestaff, and Scooby were wandering along the maze of passages trying to find the others.

Suddenly Shaggy heard the murmur of voices.

"They must be around here somewhere, Scooby," he said. "But where are they? I wonder if there is a secret chamber anywhere?"

"Secret chamber?" thought Scooby. "Whatever next?"

He sniffed around the walls trying to find the way to the kitchen for another bone and suddenly his nose touched a button which was jutting out of the wall.

Scooby's nose had pressed the button, and in a moment the wall had opened and the two detectives found themselves in the same room as their friends.

Their unexpected appearance quite threw the crooks, and before Zake could train his gun on them, Shaggy rushed at him with the pikestaff, knocking his gun out of his hand.

Freddy quickly picked it up and covered Mr Drack with it, while Shaggy and Scooby stood guard over Zake with the pikestaff.

"Quick, Daphne, phone the police, the sooner these men are under lock and key the better," cried Freddy.

So off Daphne went to find a phone, and soon the crooks and their loot were safely taken away.

"It seems such a pity to see all that money go when we're so broke," said Daphne sadly.

"Cheer up, Daphne, our money troubles are over for the moment," said Freddy. "The police have been looking for those counterfeiters for months and there was a reward for their capture."

"And we've got it," added Shaggy, flourishing a large wad of *real* dollar bills. "But you haven't told them the really exciting news yet, Freddy."

"What's that?" asked the girls eagerly.

Freddy grinned broadly. "Well, it appears that the Dracks used the castle as a cover for their activities for making money. Originally they had been hired by a food firm trying to find out if people would eat all their food if it was coloured red. The Dracks were supposed to feed folk for free and note their reactions."

"And since Scooby and I were the only ones who really liked it, we are going to appear on television promoting Ruby Rusks," grinned Shaggy. "And the pay's really good."

"Rusks?" murmured Scooby to himself. "Oh Scooby nooo. Rusks are for babies . . . dogs need bones! I'm off!"

And away Scooby fled back to the Mystery Machine where he spent the evening chewing the remains of a very old bone, only to learn later that the gang had been to the best restaurant in Vampire Valley for a slap-up feed on their reward money.

"Scooby boo hoo," howled Scooby.

"Cheer up, Scooby," cried Shaggy. "We all filled our doggy bags full of food for you before we came home. After all, it was you who opened up the secret chamber, so *you* are really the hero of our adventure in Vampire Valley."

"Scooby hooray!" cried Scooby, as he settled down to his meal. "Better late than never, I suppose!"

DEAD ENDS!

Scooby Doo is in a pickle! His friend Shaggy is stranded in a haunted house in the middle of a dark and mysterious forest. Can you help Scooby find his way through the winding paths of the forest to reach Shaggy – before the Forest Frightener does?

KNOCK KNOCK

Shaggy likes 'Knock, knock!' jokes.
Here are a few of his attempts.

Knock, knock!
Who's there?
Etta.
Etta who?
Etta Kett.

Knock, knock!
Who's there?
Caesar.
Caesar who?
Caesar jolly good fellow.

Knock, knock!
Who's there?
Jess.
Jess who?
Jess little old me.

Knock, knock!
Who's there?
Arthur.
Arthur who?
Arthur mometer is broken.

Knock, knock!
Who's there?
Hutch.
Hutch who?
Bless you!

Knock, knock!
Who's there?
Gary.
Gary who?
Gary me back to old Virginny.

Knock, knock!
Who's there?
Marcella.
Marcella who?
Marcella's full of water. Call a plumber.

HANNA-BARBERA SCOOBY DOO... WHERE ARE YOU!

NIGHT FOR A FRIGHT

SO SCOOBY WAS REMEMBERED IN THE WILL ALONG WITH FOUR OF THE COLONEL'S RELATIVES!
DAILY NEWS
FOUR PEOPLE AND A DOG INHERIT $MILLION
YEAH! I GUESS WE SHOULDN'T KNOCK A SHARE IN A MILLION BUCKS!
LET'S HURRY UP TO THE MANSION BEFORE WE'RE SOAKED!
OR SMACKED BY LIGHTNING !!
MR. CREEPS, COLONEL BEAUREGARD'S LAWYER, GREETS OUR FRIENDS...
HUMPH! SO YOU MADE IT! BRING THE "ANIMAL" INSIDE, PLEASE!
ANIMAL?!
OF ALL THE INSULTS!
HUMPH!
EVERYTHING ABOUT THIS GIVES ME THE SHIVERS FRED!
COME INTO THE LIBRARY! THE OTHER HEIRS ARE ALREADY THERE!
HEH! A LIBRARY FULLA FRESH AIRS SUITS ME TO A T-BONE!
LIKE, ER... GULP! LEAD THE WAY, SIR!

ATTENTION, PLEASE! I AM COSGOOD CREEPS, ATTORNEY FOR THE LATE COLONEL!
MY PARTNER, MR. CRAWLS, COULDN'T MAKE IT TONIGHT!
CREEPS AND CRAWLS! THEY'RE NATURALS FOR THIS JOB!
SHHHH!
ACTUALLY, I CANNOT READ THE WILL...FOR, YOU SEE, HE LEFT IT ON THIS RECORD!
NOW THEN...HEAR THE VOICE OF YOUR DEPARTED BENEFACTOR!
AHA-HA-HA-HA!
ULP! I F-FEEL LIKE DEPARTING MYSELF!
GREETIN'S, YOU ALL.....
COUSIN SIMPLE...
H-HOWDY!
NEPHEW NORVELL...
GULP!
SWEET COUSIN MALDE-HYDE
HUMPH!
COUSIN SLICKER
HEH!
AND LAST BUT NOT LEAST, MY OLD FRIEND SCOOBY DOO!
AROOO!

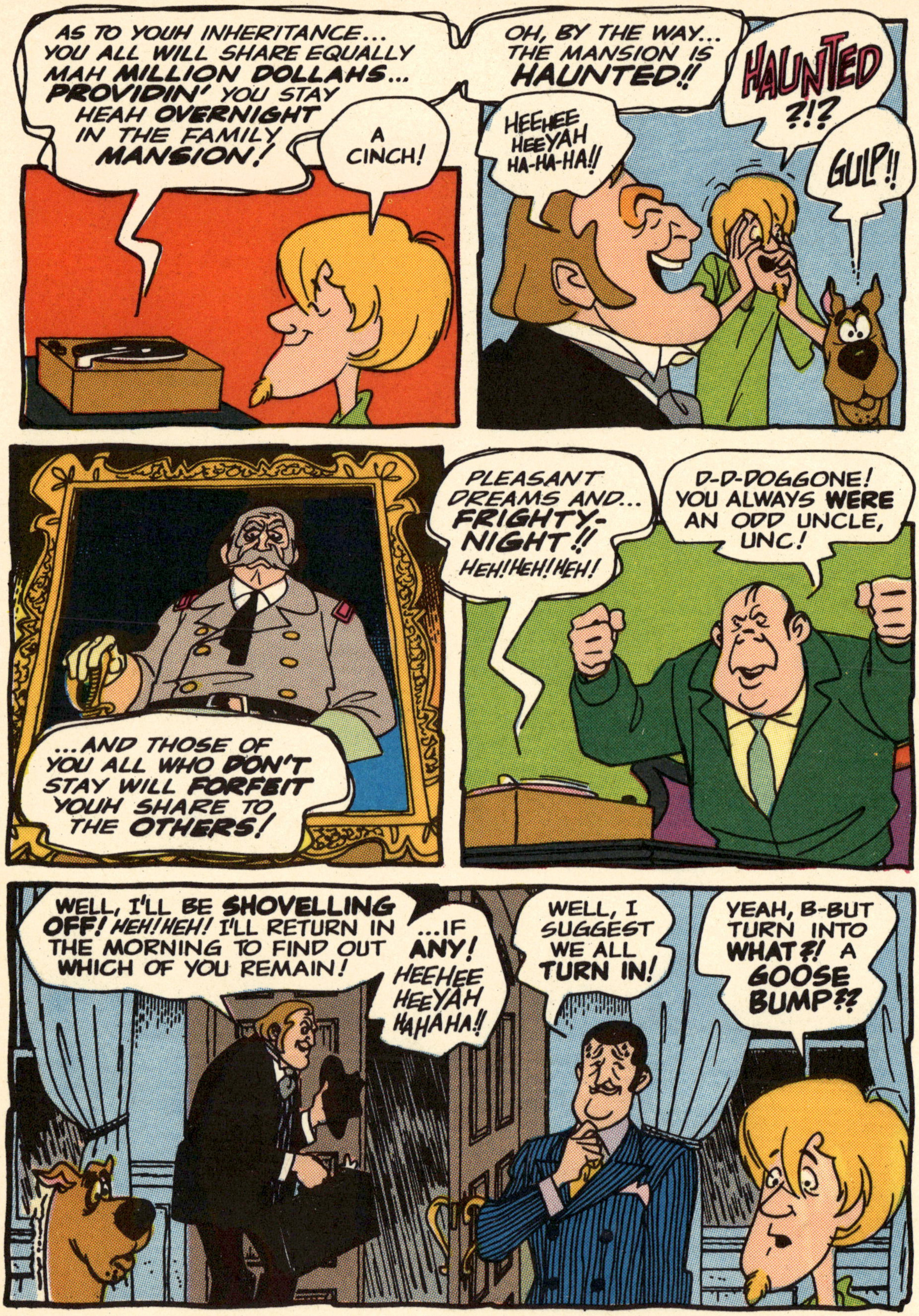
AS TO YOUH INHERITANCE... YOU ALL WILL SHARE EQUALLY MAH MILLION DOLLAHS... PROVIDIN' YOU STAY HEAH OVERNIGHT IN THE FAMILY MANSION!
A CINCH!
OH, BY THE WAY... THE MANSION IS HAUNTED!!
HEEHEE HEEYAH HA-HA-HA!!
HAUNTED ?!?
GULP!!
...AND THOSE OF YOU ALL WHO DON'T STAY WILL FORFEIT YOUH SHARE TO THE OTHERS!
PLEASANT DREAMS AND... FRIGHTY-NIGHT!! HEH! HEH! HEH!
D-D-DOGGONE! YOU ALWAYS WERE AN ODD UNCLE, UNC!
WELL, I'LL BE SHOVELLING OFF! HEH! HEH! I'LL RETURN IN THE MORNING TO FIND OUT WHICH OF YOU REMAIN!
...IF ANY! HEEHEE HEEYAH HAHAHA!!
WELL, I SUGGEST WE ALL TURN IN!
YEAH, B-BUT TURN INTO WHAT?! A GOOSE BUMP??

SO—
YAWN LET'S HIT THE SACK, MEN!
FIRST, I'M GONNA HIT THE LUNCH SACK... FOR A SHAGGY SUPER SANDWICH!
LOOKS LIKE SCOOB'S GONNA HIT THE TUB!
HIS
TUM-TE-TUM-TE-TUM! TUM-TUM-TE--WHUPS!--WHA--??
SWOOSH! SLOSH!
EEYEEOWW!!

KERTHUD!
WURF!
KLINK! KLANK! KLINK!
WHAZZAT? WHAZZAT?
EEYOWLP!!
BLA-BLA... BLABBA-BLA-BLA...
SCOOBY DOO...
SKIDDOO!!
KERASH

V-VELMA? DO YOU HEAR FEET RUNNING UP STAIRS?
I SURE DO, BUT...THERE ARE NO STAIRS NEAR HERE!
KLOMP KLOMP KLOMP
TH-THAT CLOCK IS M-M-MOVING !!
CREAK!
EEK!!
A MONSTER!!
WHA??
MONSTER?? WHERE-ZA MONSTER?? WHERE? WHERE?
PLOP! KERPLOP!
KLINK! KLANK!
YIKE! IT'S HIM! HERE HE COMES!

Continued on page 27

SCOOBY'S Crossword

Here's a ghoulish puzzle for you to solve! Solve the five clues to see what it is our friends are searching for.

Clues

Across

1 Scooby's best friend
2 The sound werewolves make
3 What vampires drink
4 The name of our canine hero
5 Someone who casts spells

Answers

Downward clue – ghost

1 Shaggy 2 Howl 3 Blood 4 Scooby 5 Witch

SPANGLES, SAWDUST... AND SCOOBY DOO!

One day the gang set off in the Mystery Machine to the small town of Starsville where Billy Beam, an old friend, was opening his big top circus that very night.

"It was great of Billy to ask us to visit," said Freddy as they pulled into the circus campsite, "but he didn't seem his usual cheerful self when I spoke to him on the phone yesterday. I'm sure that he's worried about something."

"Gee, I think you're right," replied Daphne, as she caught sight of a small stocky figure walking towards them. "It's the first time I've seen Billy looking so glum. His grin usually spreads from ear to ear."

"Or from there to there," said Shaggy, trying to make a joke. "How about being a circus star, Scooby?"

"Yeah, we could teach him to jump through hoops of fire," cried Velma. "I'm sure Scooby could do that quite easily."

"Scooby . . . noo!" cried Scooby, jumping into Shaggy's arms at the mere thought of such a thing!

"Hello, gang," said Billy as he walked up. "Am I glad to see you. Perhaps you can help me before I have to close down altogether."

"Close down?" echoed Daphne in horror. "Gee, surely not, Billy? Yours is the best circus in town, far better than Larry Lynx's circus. I suppose *he's* still around?"

"Oh, sure," replied Billy with a wry grin. "Still trying to get me to sell out to him. He comes round every time something goes wrong. It's funny how he seems to know exactly what has happened almost before it does!"

"Now *that* is interesting," murmured Freddy. "Tell me, Billy, what *has* been happening?"

"Well, someone let Jumbo the elephant loose, and he went around trampling over everything," said Billy. "He caused quite a bit of damage and brought the law round. Then someone cut the stiltsman's stilts and he fell over and broke a leg. One of the bareback riders fell off her horse and broke her wrist because the horse stumbled over a block of wood."

"I wonder who put the wood there?" said Daphne thoughtfully. "I think we'll stick around for a bit, eh, gang?"

The others nodded, and Shaggy suddenly spotted an unfamiliar figure coming out of one of the caravans.

"Who is your new clown?" he asked. "I've not seen him before."

"Oh, that's Chuckles," replied Billy. "He's not been with us very long. He's so shy that he refuses to dress any other way. He dresses as a clown all day."

"Does he?" said Freddy. "Well, I'm sure you're very busy getting ready for tonight, so leave everything to us, Billy."

"Gee, thanks, gang . . . and Scooby," said Billy. "I feel much better now that you are here."

"Are you thinking what I'm thinking?" said Daphne to Freddy as Billy went off to supervise the putting up of the circus tent.

"You mean that there's something strange about a clown walking about in make-up all day long?" replied Freddy.

Daphne nodded and added, "As if he had something to hide . . . especially his face."

"Right, I think we'd better have a look in that guy's van," said Freddy crisply. "Look, he's left the window open. Daphne, can you squeeze through it?"

"Just about," replied Daphne. "Shaggy and Scooby, stand guard outside when I let you and Velma inside."

"Warn us if Chuckles comes back. Stop him any way you can," ordered Freddy.

"Scooby too," cried the hound . . . but hiding behind Shaggy, just in case!

"What are we looking for?" asked Daphne, as she and Freddy started to look around.

"Anything suspicious," replied Freddy. "Gee, look at this!" He handed Daphne a silver necklet with a charm on it.

"What is it?" asked Velma curiously.

"It's a lynx, a silver lynx . . . and it obviously belongs to Chuckles," replied Freddy grimly.

"A lynx . . . Larry Lynx," cried Daphne. "So Larry Lynx is behind this."

"But he's running his own circus down town," said Velma. "He can't be in two places at once."

"No, but don't you remember, he has a son called Sam, who is a real good circus performer?" cried Freddy. "He can juggle, clown, even walk a tightrope. I bet my last dollar that Chuckles is Sam in disguise."

"I won't take *that* bet," grinned Daphne. "Hey, look, there's Chuckles coming back. Let's get out of here."

Fortunately for the others Shaggy had also spotted Chuckles coming back, and he and Scooby ran towards him, pretending to get in his way.

"Get out of my way, I'm in a hurry," snarled Chuckles, aiming a hard kick at Scooby.

"Scooby oow!" howled Scooby, and put out his paw, sending Chuckles sprawling.

"Let's get out of here, Scooby," cried Shaggy, and they fled to safety before Chuckles could pick himself up.

"What's our plan of action?" asked Daphne, as the gang gathered in Billy's van a little later on. "Do we confront Chuckles with the silver lynx and tell him we know who he is?"

"I don't think that would be enough evidence," said Freddy thoughtfully. "He could say he had quarrelled with his pa and wanted a new job, but that he knew that Billy would not give him one if he knew he was Larry Lynx's son. No, we shall just have to wait and watch and catch him in the act."

"How do we do that?" asked Daphne.

"By watching all the acts tonight and making sure that nothing goes wrong. In fact, Scooby and Shaggy could be in the ring themselves doing a clever dog act. I'm sure that Scooby could do it, eh, Scoob?"

"Scooby Dooo!" agreed Scooby. Being clever seemed much safer than jumping through hoops of fire.

So that evening Freddy, Velma and Daphne stationed themselves around the ring, and Chuckles fooled around as the other performers went through their acts.

He pinched one of the juggler's balls and made it appear out of his right ear and threw water all over the acrobats, making them jump down from their pyramid and chase him out of the ring.

He reappeared just as Shaggy and Scooby came into the ring and the trapeze artist started to climb the ladder.

Chuckles was carrying what appeared to be a rubber saw and started to cut down the ladder as the artiste reached the top.

The audience laughed heartily . . . but suddenly Freddy realised that the saw was real, and the girl trapeze artiste was caught half way up a swinging ladder.

"Here, catch this," called Freddy throwing her a safety rope, which allowed her to slide down to safety.

"The game's up, Sam Lynx! We know who you are and what you have been up to," shouted Daphne.

Chuckles looked around wildly. But he found the rest of the circus folk blocking the entrances out of the ring, and, with a mocking laugh, he held up his hands in surrender, and allowed himself to be led away by the law.

"Settle down, folks, the show's not over yet. The best is yet to come," cried Freddy. "Introducing Shaggy and the wonderful Scooby Doo. Ask him a question and Scooby will answer it for you. Shaggy, give them an example."

"Scooby, what colour is the sky?" asked Shaggy.

"Huh?" thought Scooby. "Scooby BLOO!" he howled to great applause.

"Right first time," replied Shaggy. "Come along, everyone, ask Scooby your questions."

"What noise do doves make?" asked a little girl on the front row.

"Scooby COOO!" replied Scooby, beginning to enjoy himself.

"What do cows say?" asked a little boy.

"Scooby MOO!" smirked Scooby, taking a bow.

"Who rows the boat?" shouted a man.

"Scooby creoow!" Scooby answered promptly.

Finally Shaggie cried, "Who is the best dog detective in the world?"

"SCOOBY DOO!" cried Scooby, looking most surprised at being asked such an easy question.

Shaggy and Scooby left the ring to a standing ovation, and Scooby began to think that the circus was the life for him . . . until Billy asked him if he was willing to be the first dog to be shot out of a cannon . . . and then Scooby just managed to answer "Scooby NOOOO!" before he ran back to the Mystery Machine and refused to come out until he was safely back home again.

After all, he was a DETECTIVE DOG . . . not a DOG CANNON!

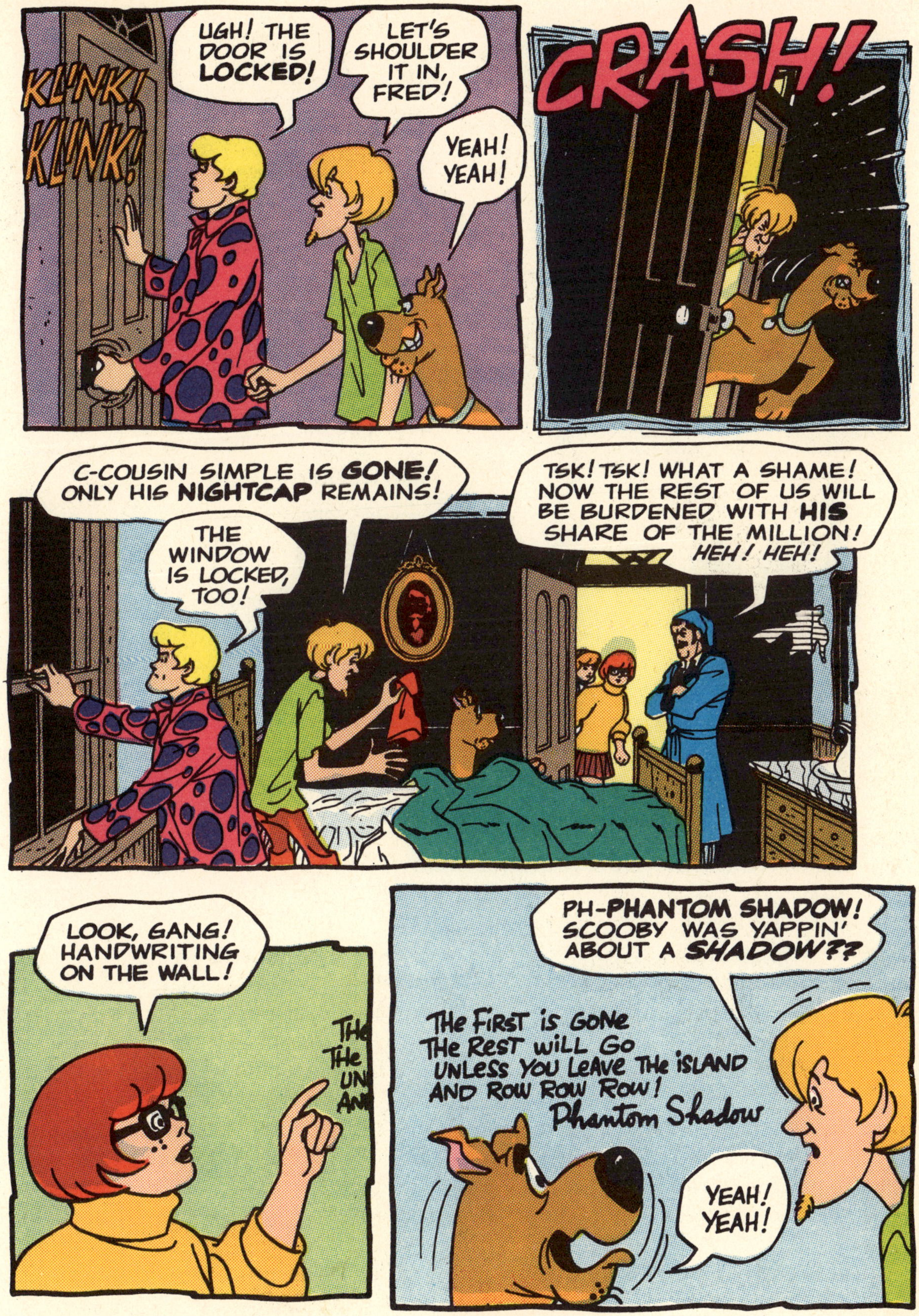
KLUNK! KLUNK!
UGH! THE DOOR IS LOCKED!
LET'S SHOULDER IT IN, FRED!
YEAH! YEAH!
CRASH!
C-COUSIN SIMPLE IS GONE! ONLY HIS NIGHTCAP REMAINS!
THE WINDOW IS LOCKED, TOO!
TSK! TSK! WHAT A SHAME! NOW THE REST OF US WILL BE BURDENED WITH HIS SHARE OF THE MILLION! HEH! HEH!
LOOK, GANG! HANDWRITING ON THE WALL!
PH-PHANTOM SHADOW! SCOOBY WAS YAPPIN' ABOUT A SHADOW??
The First is Gone
The Rest will Go
Unless You Leave The island
And Row Row Row!
Phantom Shadow
YEAH! YEAH!

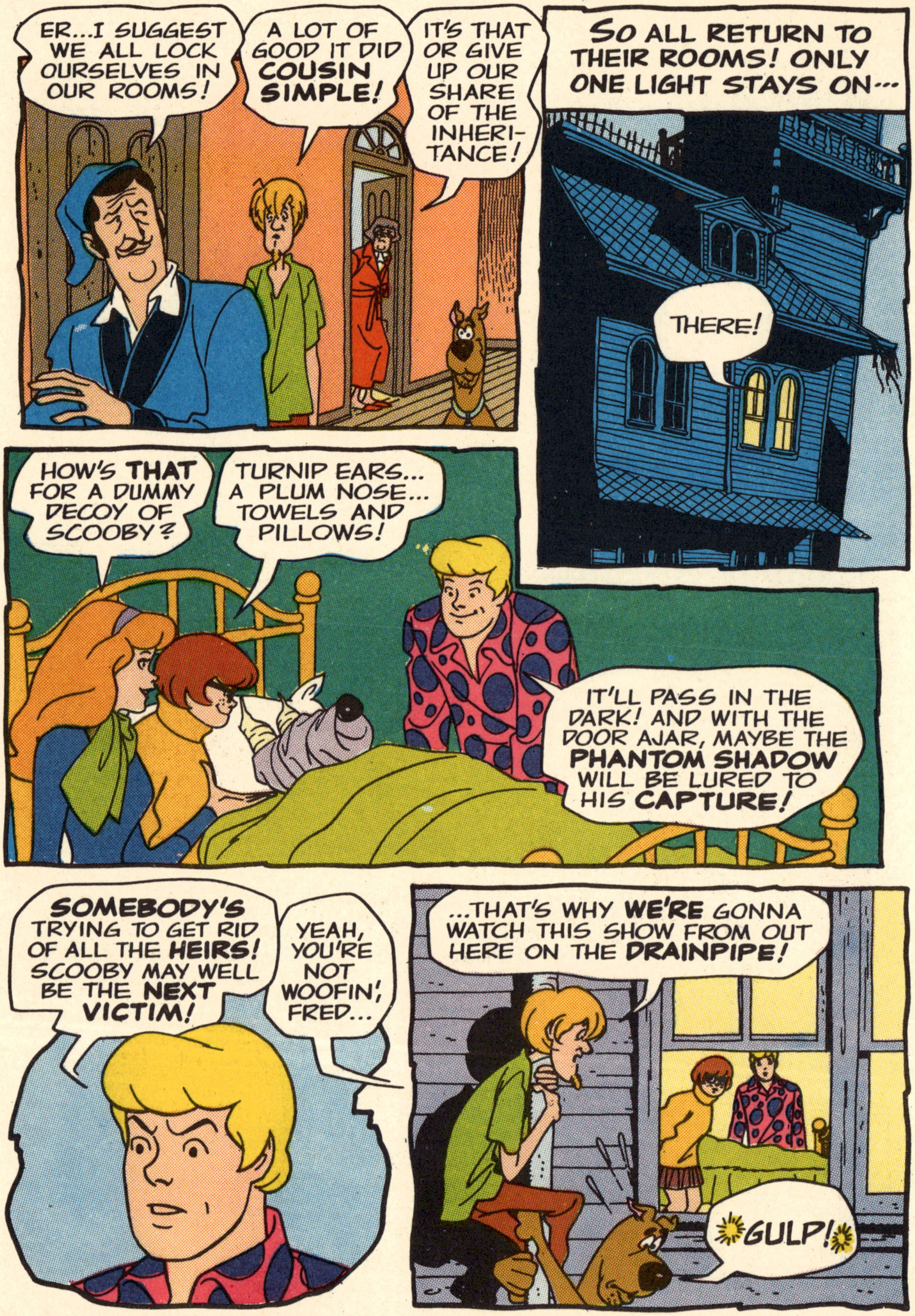
ER...I SUGGEST WE ALL LOCK OURSELVES IN OUR ROOMS!
A LOT OF GOOD IT DID COUSIN SIMPLE!
IT'S THAT OR GIVE UP OUR SHARE OF THE INHERITANCE!
SO ALL RETURN TO THEIR ROOMS! ONLY ONE LIGHT STAYS ON...
THERE!
HOW'S THAT FOR A DUMMY DECOY OF SCOOBY?
TURNIP EARS... A PLUM NOSE... TOWELS AND PILLOWS!
IT'LL PASS IN THE DARK! AND WITH THE DOOR AJAR, MAYBE THE PHANTOM SHADOW WILL BE LURED TO HIS CAPTURE!
SOMEBODY'S TRYING TO GET RID OF ALL THE HEIRS! SCOOBY MAY WELL BE THE NEXT VICTIM!
YEAH, YOU'RE NOT WOOFIN', FRED...
...THAT'S WHY WE'RE GONNA WATCH THIS SHOW FROM OUT HERE ON THE DRAINPIPE!
GULP!

HEY! AM I HAVING A PIPE DREAM...OR IS THE HOUSE MOVING?
CORRECTION, SHAGGY, YOUR PIPE IS DEPARTING! LET ME HAVE YOUR HAND...QUICKLY!
HERE, TAKE ALL TWO OF 'EM!
EEK!
VELMA!!
JUMPING JUGGERNAUTS! THE DRAINPIPE IS BENDING DOWN OVER THE CLIFF!
ULP! I DON'T HAVE A LICENSE TO FLY UPSIDE DOWN!!

KerPLOP!
WHEW! WE'RE IN A CAVE IN THE CLIFF'S SIDE!
LOOK! FOOTPRINTS GOING DEEP INSIDE!
LET'S FOLLOW THEM! YOU LEAD, SHAGGY!
I LIKE THE WAY I GOT ELECTED LEADER!
YOU'RE NOT CHICKEN, ARE YOU?
CLUCK! CLUCK! CLUCK! C'MON!
AND COCK-A-DOODLE SCOOBY DOO!
HEY! A CAVERN FULL OF CIVIL WAR RELICS! I GUESS THE COLONEL COLLECTED 'EM!
AND LOOK! THERE'S A WHOLE WAGON FULL OF CONFEDERATE UNIFORMS!
CSA

EEK! A HAUNTED UNIFORM!!
YARP!
RUN, VELMA, RUN!!
SKIDDOO !!
UGH! I LIKE THE WAY I GOT ELECTED CHICKEN-CARRIER!
OOF!
UGH! GIRLS WILL LET YOU DOWN EVERY TIME, SCOOB!
YAP !!
PLOP!
WE'VE HAD IT! THE SPOOK SUIT IS UPON US!!
FLAP! FLAP!
KAWWW!
HUH?? A CROW??
SEE, VELMA? YOU HAD NO REASON TO PANIC AND ACT THE FOOL...!

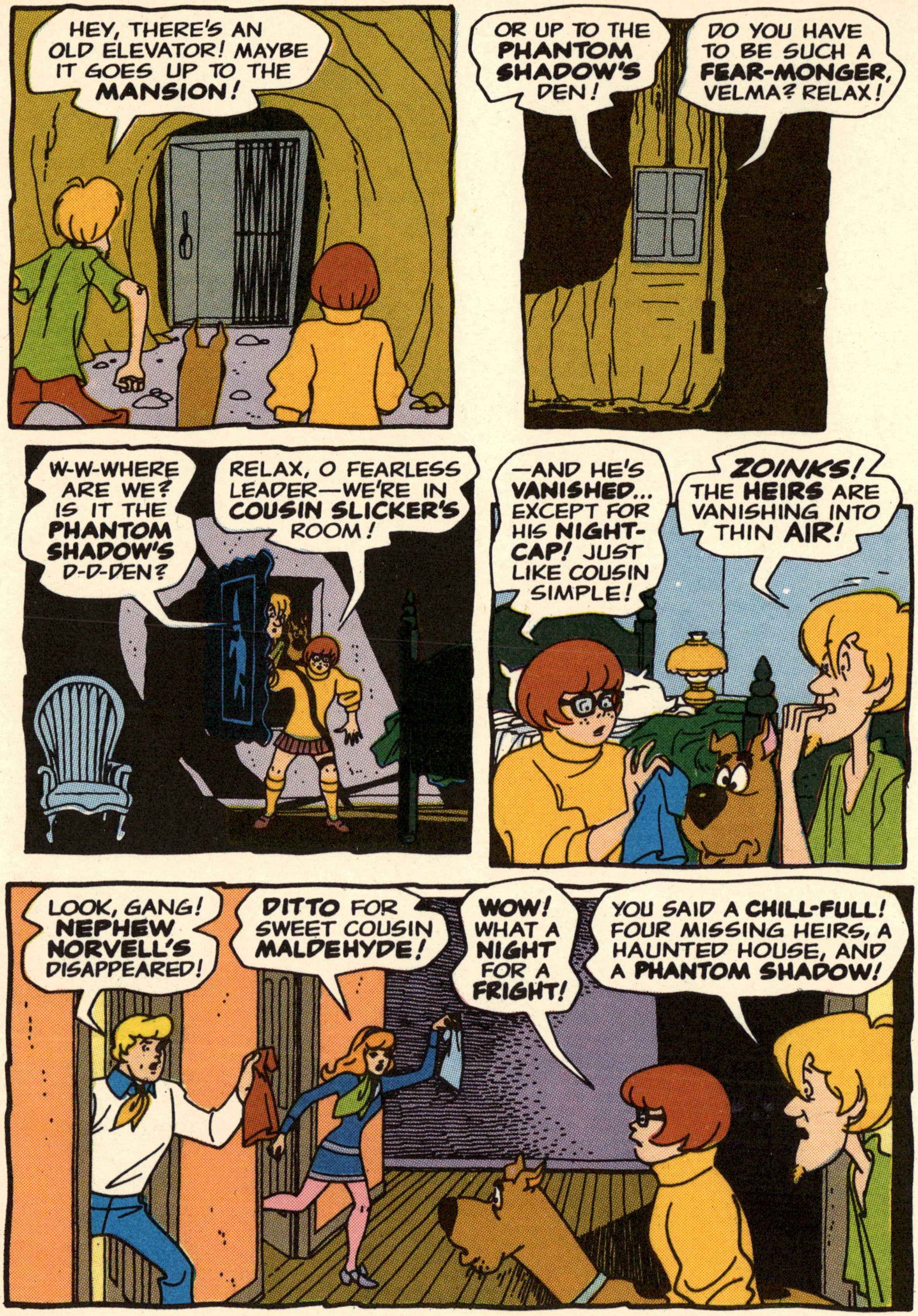
HEY, THERE'S AN OLD ELEVATOR! MAYBE IT GOES UP TO THE MANSION!
OR UP TO THE PHANTOM SHADOW'S DEN!
DO YOU HAVE TO BE SUCH A FEAR-MONGER, VELMA? RELAX!
W-W-WHERE ARE WE? IS IT THE PHANTOM SHADOW'S D-D-DEN?
RELAX, O FEARLESS LEADER—WE'RE IN COUSIN SLICKER'S ROOM!
—AND HE'S VANISHED... EXCEPT FOR HIS NIGHT-CAP! JUST LIKE COUSIN SIMPLE!
ZOINKS! THE HEIRS ARE VANISHING INTO THIN AIR!
LOOK, GANG! NEPHEW NORVELL'S DISAPPEARED!
DITTO FOR SWEET COUSIN MALDEHYDE!
WOW! WHAT A NIGHT FOR A FRIGHT!
YOU SAID A CHILL-FULL! FOUR MISSING HEIRS, A HAUNTED HOUSE, AND A PHANTOM SHADOW!

SAY, WITH THE OTHER HEIRS GONE, SCOOBY WILL INHERIT THE WHOLE MILLION BY HIMSELF!
YAY! OL' SCOOB'S A JOLLY RICH BOW-WOW!
SCOOBY DOO-O-O!
HOLD IT, HOLD IT! THIS IS NO TIME FOR PREMATURE CELEBRATIONS!
LIKE, WHY NOT ?
LOOK WHAT'S HAPPENED TO THE DUMMY DECOY OF SCOOBY WE SET UP!
ZOWIE! IT'S ALL TORN UP! THE STUFFIN'S ARE OUT OF THE PILLOW!
YOWLP!
POOR SCOOBY! HE'S THE LONE SURVIVING HEIR...BUT NOW HE'S ALSO THE LONE OBJECT OF THE PHANTOM SHADOW'S WRATH!
WE'VE GOTTA HIDE HIM IN A GOOD, SAFE PLACE TILL MORNING!
HMMM

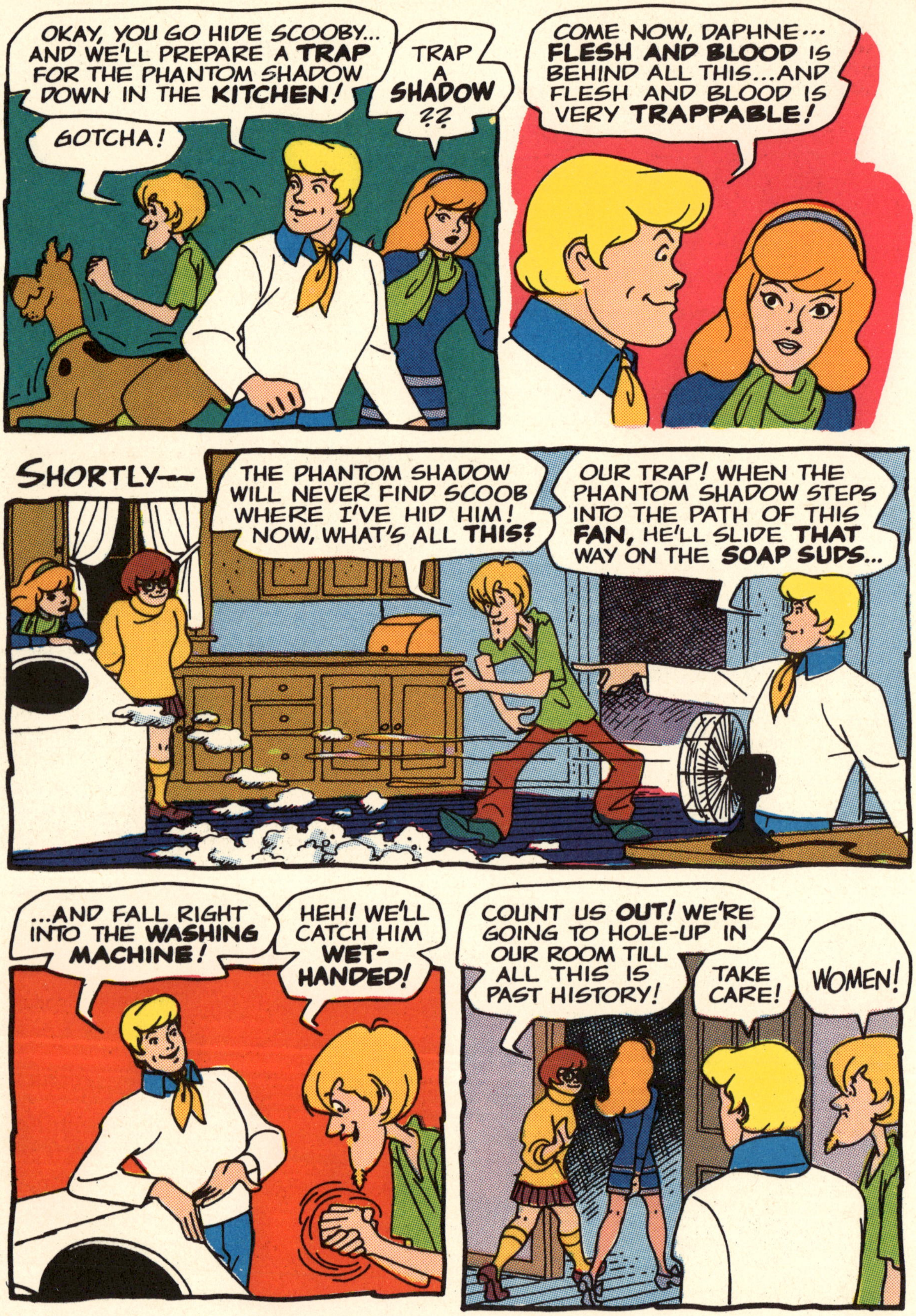
OKAY, YOU GO HIDE SCOOBY... AND WE'LL PREPARE A TRAP FOR THE PHANTOM SHADOW DOWN IN THE KITCHEN!
GOTCHA!
TRAP A SHADOW ??
COME NOW, DAPHNE... FLESH AND BLOOD IS BEHIND ALL THIS...AND FLESH AND BLOOD IS VERY TRAPPABLE!
SHORTLY---
THE PHANTOM SHADOW WILL NEVER FIND SCOOB WHERE I'VE HID HIM! NOW, WHAT'S ALL THIS?
OUR TRAP! WHEN THE PHANTOM SHADOW STEPS INTO THE PATH OF THIS FAN, HE'LL SLIDE THAT WAY ON THE SOAP SUDS...
...AND FALL RIGHT INTO THE WASHING MACHINE!
HEH! WE'LL CATCH HIM WET-HANDED!
COUNT US OUT! WE'RE GOING TO HOLE-UP IN OUR ROOM TILL ALL THIS IS PAST HISTORY!
TAKE CARE!
WOMEN!

Continued on page 48

ESCAPE from the SPOOK!

Scooby and the gang are running away from the Spook! Can you help them to get back to the Mystery Machine before the Spook gets there? To play this game, you will need some counters, one for each person, and a dice. You must throw a six to start, and if you land on an obstacle square you must follow the instructions. The winner is the person who reaches the Mystery Machine first, and you must throw the exact number to win!

FALL IN THE SWAMP—
MISS A TURN
GO BACK 5 PLACES
GO ON 2 SPACES
THROW AGAIN
MISS A TURN
GET LOST IN THE FOG—
MISS A TURN
GO BACK 2
THROW AGAIN
SLIP ON THE MUD—
GO BACK 2
GO ON 2 SPACES

A MONSTER COLLAGE

Here's a monster for you – one that Scooby Doo and his friends might easily encounter on one of their adventures.

To make this fearsome-looking creature you will need: some egg boxes cardboard, scissors, glue, paints and crayons.

Take a large sheet of thick paper or card, and draw on it a picture of the fiercest monster you can think of, filling the whole sheet.

Separate the egg boxes into single cups and stick these onto your drawing, as close together as possible, and following the outline as near as you can. To fill in any gaps that are left, tear the remaining pieces of egg box into small strips, and stick them on to look like scales.

Decide how many eyes you want your monster to have, and paint them white with a black middle. Then choose your favourite monster colour, and paint the rest of him, remembering to paint the sides of the cups. If you have left a gap for a mouth, paint the inside black, and fill it with two strips of cardboard teeth – suitably fang-coloured, of course!

Waiter: What would you like to eat, sir?
Ghost customer: Spooketti, please, then a ghoulash.

GHOSTLY GUFFAWS

Patient: I can't see very well these days.
Optician: Don't worry, I'll measure you for a new pair of spooktacles.

Fan: Dracula, where do you get all your great jokes from?
Dracula: From my crypt writer, of course.

Adult ghost: What are you going to do when you grow up?
Young ghost: I like the seaside. I'm going to join the Ghost Guard.

What do you call a wicked old woman who lives by the sea?
A sandwitch.

Happy Birthday Scooby Doo!

At any other time of the year Scooby would have been extremely annoyed if the gang had kept going into a huddle and whispering together, and then shutting up when he approached . . . but not today. Scooby knew what all the whispers and giggles were about . . . the gang were planning his birthday surprise, and it was sure to be good.

But this year Scooby was to have a birthday he would remember for a long time . . .

"Now is everything going according to plan?" asked Daphne. "Velma, have you ordered that special cake from *Goodies for Doggies*?"

"Sure, we pick it up tomorrow, along with a giant pack of Scooby Snacks," said Velma, peering short-sightedly through her glasses.

"And we'll pick up that special diamante collar at *Dogs' Delights* at the same time," said Freddy. "I know Scooby is real fond of his Scooby Doo badge, but this one will be great for those special occasions. Wasn't it lucky that the shop just had one with SD picked out in . . ."

"Best imitation glass," chuckled Daphne. "But it does look like real diamonds . . . even Scooby won't be able to tell the difference."

And, of course, our favourite detective

hound did think they were great. He'd actually spotted them in the window and had nudged Shaggy and Freddy along until they had seen them too. He wasn't taking any chances about getting a plastic bone that squeaked, like he got last year!

So Scooby allowed himself to be taken for a walk by Shaggy while the others went shopping.

Velma and Daphne picked up the cake without any trouble, but as they passed *Dogs' Delight* they noticed that Freddy seemed to be arguing with the assistant and another swarthy man who was also a customer.

As the girls entered the shop Freddy was saying, politely but firmly, "I'm sorry, but this is a very special collar for a very special dog. If the assistant had promised it to you, hard luck, I've bought it and I'm not handing it back. Surely the shop can get you another one like it . . ."

"There isn't another one like it, you young fool!" snarled the man. Then, seeing Freddy's look of amazement, he went on in slightly more genial tones, "It's for my old mother's dog, you see. She'll be heartbroken not to be able to give it to her pet tomorrow. Come on, son, what do you say?"

Freddy hesitated and looked at the girls for advice. He opened his mouth to offer the dog collar to the man, when suddenly the door burst open and a hardfaced brassy blonde strode in.

"Ain't you got that dog collar yet?" she demanded. "Hurry up, or you'll be in trouble. Diamond Dan doesn't like being kept waiting."

"Is that your mother?" asked Daphne sweetly. "Charming old lady, I don't think! Come on, gang, let's get out of here."

Freddy and the girls rushed out of the shop, quickly followed by the blonde and the swarthy guy at their heels.

"Get the collar!" ordered the blonde to

another man who was sitting in a car outside.

But as he waş getting out, Scooby and Shaggy were just trotting up.

"My cake," thought Scooby as he spotted the large box, and he bounded up to Daphne, dragging Shaggy behind him. The blonde and the two crooks got caught up in the lead, and as they stumbled and tumbled about, Freddy and the girls rushed into a theatrical costumier's shop, and hid behind some large baskets and rows of clothes.

A moment later Shaggy and Scooby appeared and, as the blonde and her confederates passed by the shop window Scooby jumped into a basket and hid there shivering, while Shaggy popped a policeman's helmet on and stood quite still.

"They must be around here somewhere, Jake," said the blonde to the swarthy man. "You two take that side of the street and I'll try the drug store here. Remember, we must get that collar back at all costs, got it?"

"Sure, Lil, sure," said Jake, and Daphne almost gave away their hiding place as she saw Jake produce a gun and check the bullets.

Scooby, who was watching through a crack in the basket, almost fainted with fright.

"Scooby OOOH!" he gulped.

"It's OK, they've gone, now we can see what all the fuss was about," said Freddy, as he gazed down at the collar. "Why should a diamond thief want a paste diamond dog collar?"

"If it *is* paste," said Daphne significantly.

"All that glitters is sometimes not glass."

"Well, there's one way to find out," said Freddy as he took out a large mirror from a basket of props. *"Real* diamonds cut glass!"

"Scooby OOOH!" gasped Scooby as he watched Freddy drag the collar along the mirror.

"Just look at that!" breathed Velma, gazing in amazement at the long scratch all over the mirror. "Gee, that means . . ."

"That this really is a diamond collar!" cried Daphne. "But how did they get there in the first place?"

"I think this answers your question, Daphne," said Shaggy, picking up a crumpled newspaper from the floor. "Someone stole a bagful of diamonds from a well-known diamond merchant's car in the last few days. They must have hit on the idea of a dog collar for easy transport. The guy in the shop must have been in on the deal, but unfortunately, he sold Freddy the wrong collar by mistake."

"Lucky for us," grinned Freddy. "Now all we have to do is get this collar to the police."

"Yeah, that's ALL!" replied Daphne dryly. "How do you suggest we go about it with those three prowling about outside?"

"And one of them with a gun," added Shaggy unhappily.

"Scooby gun!" whimpered Scooby, trying to creep back into the basket.

"I think . . ." began Freddy.

"You think too much, son, that's your trouble," said a voice behind him. "I saw how those stupid guys tried to get back the collar. I was watching from the window of the block over the street. I've just dealt with Wally the fence. *He* won't make any mistakes any more!"

Turning round, the gang saw a flashily dressed man smiling grimly at them. He wore several rings on his fingers and a diamond tiepin.

"Diamond Dan, I presume?" said Freddy calmly.

"Yeah, clever of you to guess," sneered the man. "Now, hand over that dog collar or you won't have a dog to wear any collar."

Poor Scooby jumped into Shaggy's arms as Diamond Dan produced a flick knife and advanced towards them.

"Right, here you are," cried Freddy, and he threw the collar at Diamond Dan, hitting him smartly on the wrist, causing him to drop the knife.

As the diamond thief hopped about holding his wrist in pain, Freddy picked up the knife and started towards the door . . . only to stop at the sight of Jake and Lil the blonde coming through the door.

"Stop them!" ordered Diamond Dan, as the gang looked around for a means of escape.

And so a merry chase began. In and out of the rooms everyone ran, turning and whirling, knocking into everything and everyone. Jake and Freddy clambered over dummies wearing various costumes, Lil chased Velma into the window, but she escaped because Lil had to pretend to be a model when two people stopped to look in the window.

Shaggy and Scooby kept falling over everyone, and Diamond Dan tried to push Shaggy in a cupboard. But Scooby, searching for somewhere to hide, knocked Dan over, causing him to stumble and enabling Shaggy to make his escape.

Meanwhile Daphne was desperately

searching all the baskets in the hope of finding a dummy gun with which to bluff the thieves into giving themselves up.

"Hurray, I've found one at last!" she murmured, as she found a policeman's outfit, complete with truncheon and handcuffs.

"Yeah, but mine's a real one," sneered a mocking voice behind her.

Whirling around, Daphne found herself staring down into the barrel of Jake's gun as he also trained it on Freddy and Velma, with Diamond Dan and his cronies standing behind them.

"Give me that collar!" he cried to Freddy. "Quickly, now, there's been enough foolin' about."

Freddy sighed and looked down at the collar . . . and then he looked down at the floor.

It was covered with pins which had been used by the theatrical dressmaker when she altered costumes which did not fit customers properly. And near the pins lay . . .

From the corner of his eye Freddy saw Shaggy and Scooby hiding behind a large cupboard.

"Scooby, pick up that magnet," ordered Freddy.

"For a Scooby Snack . . . a whole bagful!" added Shaggy, as Scooby hesitated.

That was one offer Scooby just could not refuse!

As the thieves watched in bewilderment, Scooby picked up the magnet and tossed it to Freddy who caught it neatly . . . and aimed it at Jake's gun.

The gun flew straight to the magnet and stuck fast.

"Quickly, Velma, phone the police, I'll keep these customers happy until the law arrives," snapped Freddy, as Daphne used two sets of handcuffs to lock up the thieves.

"Well done, Scooby," cried Shaggy, hugging him hard. "You're a real hero. It was your quick thinking that saved the day. You'll get a reward for this!"

"But I'm afraid we'll have to get you another 'diamond' collar. This one will have to be returned to the diamond merchant."

"Let's not bother about a diamond collar. Scooby looks better with his own Scooby Doo badge," said Shaggy. "We'll buy him a year's supply of special Scooby Snacks instead."

"NOW you're talking," thought Scooby in delight. "I never did think that diamonds were a dog's best friend. Scooby Snacks are a far better present."

And so Scooby had a really good birthday . . . apart from the fact that when he cut the cake, he also cut off part of Shaggy's beard!

Oh, Scooby Doo! But happy birthday all the same!

SEND A SECRET MESSAGE

Scooby Doo and his friends know all about secret codes and messages. Do you?

When you have a very special message to send to someone, and you don't want anyone else to know about it, why not try sending it in one of these very secret ways?

MIRROR WRITING

That looks very strange, doesn't it? But just try holding this page up to a mirror, and then what do you see? The message 'meet me at the hollow tree' shows in the mirror quite clearly.

To make a mirror-writing message, all you have to do is write the words backwards. This takes quite a bit of practice, and you may make a few mistakes at first, so you should check each word after you've written it by holding it up to your mirror.

And make sure that your friend knows the secret of how to read your message!

INVISIBLE WORDS

Invisible writing sounds rather mysterious, doesn't it? But it's really very simple.

All you'll need is a lemon or an onion, a pen with a clean nib, and a sheet of paper. Squeeze the lemon or the onion until you have collected quite a bit of juice in a bowl. Dip your pen into the juice, and write the message on a piece of paper.

Leave the ink to dry, and when it does you'll find your message has completely disappeared.

When your friend receives it, he or she will have to hold it a little way above a radiator or lamp, and as the warm air rises, the message will reappear.

A SIMPLE CODE

One very effective method of sending secret messages is to send them in code. Spies have to know a lot about codes, and the ones they use are often very, very difficult to 'break'.

But for your first coded messages, here's a very simple code, which is easy to use. Each letter of the alphabet has a number underneath it, like this:

A	B	C	D	E	F	G	H	I	J	K	L	M
1	2	3	4	5	6	7	8	9	10	11	12	13

N	O	P	Q	R	S	T	U	V	W	X	Y	Z
14	15	16	17	18	19	20	21	22	23	24	25	26

So the same message that we wrote in 'Mirror Writing', would read like this in code:

13 5 5 20 13 5 1 20 20 8 5 8 15 12 12 15 23 20 18 5 5

When you've had a bit of practice at writing in code, you can begin to make up codes of your own. And then your messages really will be secret!

YEEEEK!! THE PHANTOM SHADOW IS AT THE WINDOW!!
H-HE IS?!?
OWOOOO-ARROOOOO
M-MERCY!
FRED! SHAGGY! HALLLP!
I'M GETTIN' MY HIDE OUT OF HERE!!
HEY, I WONDER WHO'S HOWLING? HE HAS THE STRANGEST ACCENT!
AWOOO! AND BOW-WOO, TOO!
WE COULD USE ANOTHER DOG AROUND HERE! THE PEOPLE AREN'T DOING TOO WELL!
AWOOOO

SCOOBY !!
WHA??
WATCH IT! YOU'RE IN OUR PHANTOM SHADOW TRAP!!
???
TSK! TSK! TSK!
YIPE YIPE YIPE YIPE YIPE YIPE YIPE
WELL, SO FAR THE TRAP WORKS AS PLANNED!
kerBLUMP!
SLAM!
SPLOSH SLOSH SPLOSH
AN AUTOMATIC BATH? THE OLD-FASHIONED KIND WAS HUMILIATIN' ENOUGH!

THIS IS THE LAST STRAW FOR SCOOBY!
RRROWLF!
YIKES! HE'S FLIPPED HIS LID!
...AND THE WASHER'S LID, TOO!
SHADOW-SHMADOW!! AARGGGHHH!!
OH-OH! YOU KNOW WHAT, FRED?
SCOOBY'S GOING AFTER THE PHANTOM SHADOW NOW!
...LIKE, DOWN SOME STAIRS BEHIND THE ELDERLY-TYPE CLOCK!
HOLD IT, SCOOB... YOU'RE UNARMED!
BUT I'M TERRIBLY WELL-TOOTHED!!
GROWF!

C'MON, FRED, WE CAN'T LET SCOOB GO IT ALONE!
HUH? NO KLINKIN' SHADOW AROUND THE COAL PILE NOW!
WOW! A GHOSTLY BONE!!
WELL, THAT DOESN'T SCARE ME!!
ARRGGHH
SNAP!
YAP! IT WAS A TRAP!!

MEANWHILE—
HEY, LOOK, DAPHNE! A BIG OLD PIPE ORGAN! I WONDER IF IT STILL PLAYS!
EH? LOOK AT THE SILLY NOTE!
FEED the organ
HOW CAN YOU FEED AN ORGAN?
BY PUTTING NOTES IN ITS PIPES MAYBE ??
WELL, IT DOES WORK! SOME INSTRUMENT!
ULP! DO YOU HAVE TO PLAY A FUNERAL DIRGE, VELMA?
BUT...THERE MUST BE SOME SPECIAL SIGNIFICANCE TO THIS NOTE! HMMM...
FEED the organ
IN THE BASEMENT, SCOOBY CONTINUES HIS STRUGGLE WITH THE GHOSTLY BONE...
WHA?? THE BONE HAS STRINGS!!

H-HELP! I LOST MY BALANCE!!
ANOTHER PHANTOM SHADOW! A LA PUPPETEER!
KERRASH!
YOWLP!
ALL RIGHT!! THAT DOES IT!! NO MORE NICE PHANTOM SHADOW!!
GRRR! C'MERE, YOU CUR!!
THERE'S A TIME TO RUN ...AND THIS IS IT!!
ONE DOWN AND OUT...BUT THE OTHER'S BOUND TO CATCH SCOOBY!
S-STOP HIM, FRED! YOU'RE SORTA TOUGH!

ULP! H-HERE COMES TROUBLE!
SAY, I THINK I KNOW WHAT 'FEED THE ORGAN' MEANS!
I'LL HIT THE NOTES F-E-E-D AND SEE WHAT HAPPENS!
VELMA! THOSE NOTES OPENED A TRAP DOOR IN THE FLOOR!
YAHHHH!!
SCOOBY DOO!!
AND WE'VE SCOOBY-BOOBY-TRAPPED THE PHANTOM SHADOW!
CORRECTION, VELMA! YOU CAUGHT ONE OF THE PHANTOM SHADOWS! WE'VE GOT THE OTHER ...AND LOOK WHO IT IS!
MR. CREEPS, THE LAWYER! BY ELIMINATING THE HEIRS, HE HOPED TO KEEP THE INHERITANCE HIMSELF!
BUT... WHO'S THIS ONE?

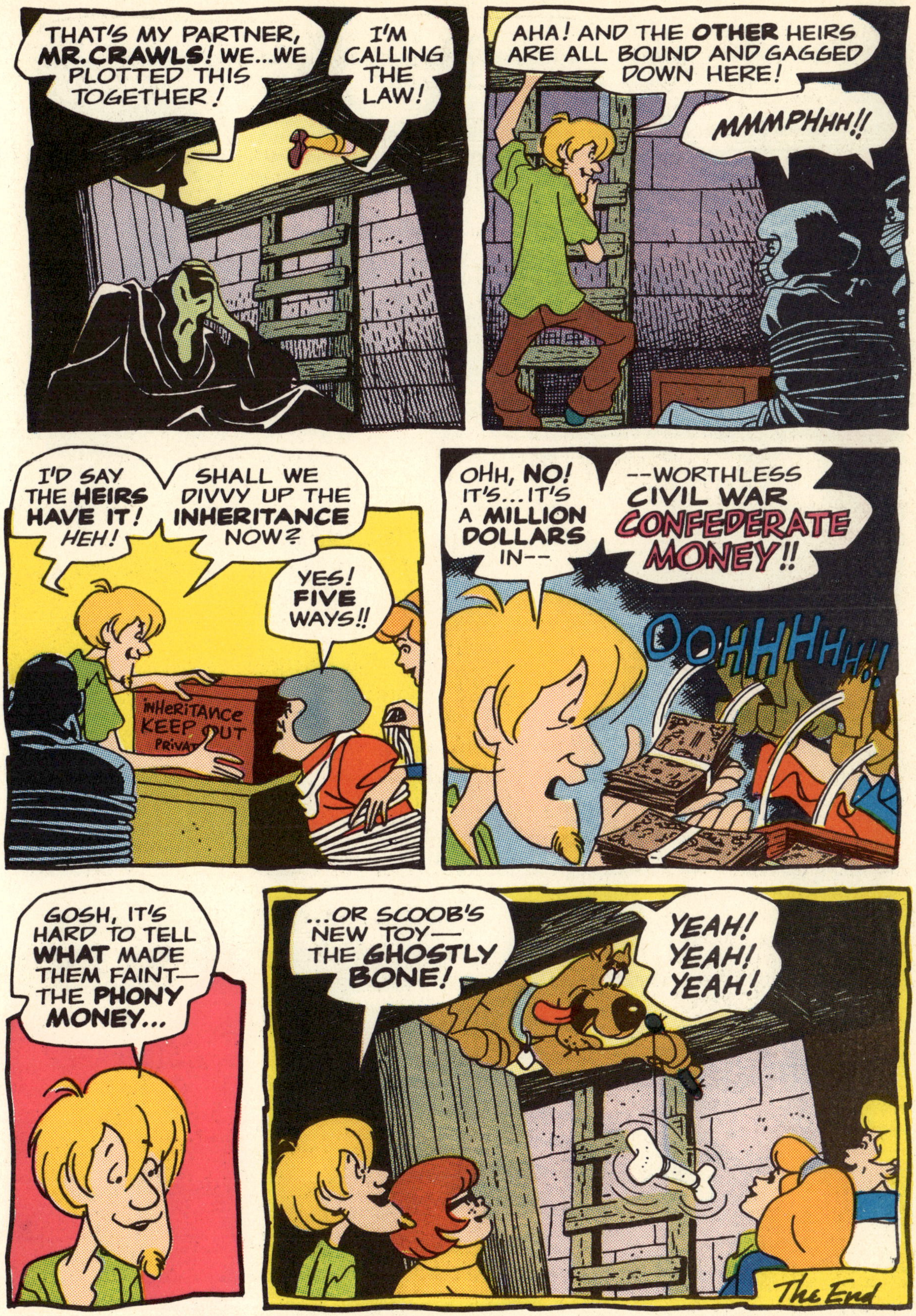
THAT'S MY PARTNER, MR. CRAWLS! WE...WE PLOTTED THIS TOGETHER!
I'M CALLING THE LAW!
AHA! AND THE OTHER HEIRS ARE ALL BOUND AND GAGGED DOWN HERE!
MMMPHHH!!
I'D SAY THE HEIRS HAVE IT! HEH!
SHALL WE DIVVY UP THE INHERITANCE NOW?
YES! FIVE WAYS!!
INHERITANCE KEEP OUT
OHH, NO! IT'S...IT'S A MILLION DOLLARS IN--
--WORTHLESS CIVIL WAR CONFEDERATE MONEY!!
OOHHHHHH!!
GOSH, IT'S HARD TO TELL WHAT MADE THEM FAINT— THE PHONY MONEY...
...OR SCOOB'S NEW TOY— THE GHOSTLY BONE!
YEAH! YEAH! YEAH!
The End

Ghostly GIGGLES!

Where does Dracula stay when he visits New York?
The Vampire State Building.

Why are ghosts like the driving rain?
Because they always seem to come in sheets.

What did the mother ghost say to the baby ghost?
Don't spook until you're spooken to.

What do ghosts wear on their feet?
Ghoul-oshes.

Where does a witch go first when she's going on a journey?
To the broom cupboard.

Scooby Doo, Phantom Hound

"Hi, Daphne, why so glum? Is your letter so bad?" asked Freddie as he watched his friend reading her morning mail with a troubled frown on her face.

"It's from old Granny Appleseed," replied Daphne, looking up. "You remember, gang, that nice old lady we once met from Appletree County? It seems that she's been having trouble . . . someone wants her out of her cottage!"

"I'd have thought she'd have been quite glad about that," responded Velma, pushing her glasses back on her nose. "From what she told us it was water from the well and oil lamps for lighting . . . and she's no spring chicken."

Hearing the last two words Scooby raised his head from off Shaggy's knee and then, realising that there was no food about, promptly closed his eyes again.

"Scooby noo!" he thought sadly. "We're not having lunch yet."

"That's true," Freddie said in answer to Velma, "but it all depends if the price is right."

"Well, this one certainly isn't. Look!" said Daphne, and she passed over Granny's letter for Freddie to read.

"You can say that again," agreed Freddie with a whistle. "I think we'd all better get down to Appletree County and sort out this whole thing before it gets any worse."

"Oh, that's a swell idea, let's get going!" cried Velma. "Come on, gang!"

"What's the hurry?" asked Shaggy, as he searched his pockets in the hope of finding a piece of gum. "Shouldn't we eat first?"

"We could do," agreed Daphne. "But think of Granny's apple dumplings and apple turnovers . . ."

". . . To say nothing of her turkey and

apple stuffing pies," added Freddie with a grin. "And she's sure to have a big juicy bone for Scooby . . . remember how fond she was of him?"

Scooby raised his head, wide awake now . . . *he* remembered Granny *and* her bones! What were the gang waiting for?

"Scooby goo now," he howled.

"Well, what are we waiting for?" cried

Shaggy, his mouth already watering at the thought of all that delicious food!

The others grinned at each other. They could read those two like a book . . . a cookery book!

"If we set off now, we should be there by tonight," said Freddie, looking at his watch.

So everyone piled into the Mystery Machine and soon they were speeding out of town towards Appletree County.

"Granny Appleseed's cottage certainly is a wreck," exclaimed Daphne as they drew up in front of the gate, which was hanging crookedly from its hinges. "She said it was old and that she had no money for repairs, but I never thought that it would have been as bad as this."

But as Granny heard their voices, she came out. "Oh, thank goodness it's you. I thought it was those two men back again," she cried, her face wreathed in smiles as she recognised the gang. "I knew that you'd be down as soon as you got my letter. I've got bacon and apple stew in the oven all ready, with apple and honey dumplings to follow . . . and I asked the butcher for a specially big bone for Scooby."

"Scooby thank yooou!" cried Scooby, bounding into the cottage, quickly followed by Shaggy, eager to sit down to supper.

"Now, tell us all about it," said Daphne at the end of the meal as Granny poured them coffee from a steaming pot.

"Well, such strange things have been happening since I refused to sell my home to those two men," replied Granny, her eyes a little afraid as she talked.

"What kind of things?" asked Freddie gently.

"I keep hearing strange voices urging me to leave and strange tapping noises as if someone is walking about in the attic. But when I go up, there's no one there," said the little old lady. "I'm beginning to think that this place is haunted."

"Haunted ooh," whimpered Scooby.

"H-h-haunted?" echoed Shaggy, and he and Scooby clung together for comfort.

"Well, we're here now . . . and we just like dealing with *ghosts,* if they *are* ghosts," said Daphne firmly. "Tell us more about the two men who called on you."

"Well, dear, they're called Wingle and Dingle. Sound like a burlesque act, don't they?" replied Granny, managing a weak little smile. "Said they couldn't bear to see me living in such squalor and would buy me out . . . but the money they offered wouldn't buy me anything better than here!"

"You're right there, Granny," agreed Velma, nodding her head in agreement.

"Yes, but when I refused to sell, they turned very nasty," went on Granny sadly. "They said that I would be very sorry."

"Have they been back?" asked Freddie.

"They're coming back later tonight," admitted Granny. "But I did once think that I saw them hanging about . . . just before the noises and tapping started."

"Hmm, that's very interesting," murmured Freddie thoughtfully. "Do you mind if we look around, Granny?"

"Help yourselves, gang," replied Granny. "No, girls, leave the dishes. You go and help the boys."

"Right, Shaggy and I will look outside, you girls look in the attic," ordered Freddie. "Look for anything unusual . . . like a ghost!" he ended with a chuckle.

"Ghost!" murmured Shaggy. "Do you have to keep using that word?"

"Scooby noo like either," thought Scooby as he followed the girls upstairs.

About half an hour later the gang met up again and compared notes.

"Found anything?" asked Freddie.

"Scooby ooh-yes," howled Scooby.

"Scooby knocked over an old washing jug and bowl . . . and what do you think we found?" cried Velma. "A tape recorder!"

"Good old Scooby Doo!" cried Shaggy. "And we found something too . . . a ladder hidden in the shrubbery."

"That's the way they got into the attic, and those were the footsteps Granny Appleseed heard," gasped Velma. "And the voices came from the tape. But what are we going to do now?"

"I've though of that," grinned Freddie. "They want a ghost . . . so we'll give them one . . . Scooby!"

"Scooby whoo!" wailed Scooby. "I'm no ghost . . . Freddie, what do you mean?"

"How can Scooby be a ghost?" cried Shaggy, his arms around his pet.

"Easily, with a can of special phosphorus paint . . . harmless to animals, but which will glow in the dark. I just happen to have one in the Mystery Machine," said Freddie with a wide grin.

"But what happens then?" asked Velma, as Freddie started to cover a rather protesting Scooby. "How will a ghostly Scooby help?"

"Leave everything to me, but back up the story I tell," said Freddie, "and remember about the emperor's new clothes . . . only this is in reverse."

"You're beginning to lose me, Freddie," said Daphne.

"Me too," admitted Velma.

Shaggy and Scooby didn't even speak . . . one look in the mirror had scared Scooby to death . . . and it was *his* reflection!

"Scooby noo!" he howled.

"Scooby is our emperor," explained Freddie, "our ghost emperor. But when he appears you must pretend not to see him. Got it?"

"Not really," the girls said, and Granny and Shaggy looked very bewildered.

"Hide under the table, Scooby, until you hear me tapping," said Freddie. "Then come out. Listen, the men are here now. Let them in, Granny."

The two men looked very surprised and rather dismayed to see the gang. But Wingle said, genially enough, "I hope you've persuaded Granny to sell to us. It's rather a weird place, supposed to be haunted, I believe."

"Yeah, yeah, haunted," agreed his partner.

"Oh yes, it is haunted, by a vicious silver dog," replied Freddie. "Several people have seen it . . . but do you know, it's a strange thing, but it's only seen by rascals and rogues. Apparently it's a warning to them to give up their bad ways or they are chased for the rest of their lives by the phantom hound."

"I've never heard such rubbish in my life," cried Wingle. "Now, old lady . . ."

But suddenly he stopped in sheer fright, because just then Freddie had knocked on the table and out came Scooby.

"Hello. Howddo!" he howled, trying to lick Wingle's hand.

"The hound . . . the phantom hound!" shrieked Wingle. "Can't you see it? It's trying to bite me! Get it off!"

"Hound, what hound, Mr Wingle?" cried Granny Appleseed gravely. "I can't see any hound. Can you, boys and girls?"

The gang shook their heads solemnly

and Scooby looked sadly at Shaggy.

"Oh, Scooby . . . poor yoou, boo-hoo!" he howled.

But to Wingle and Dingle it seemed like a warning of instant death.

"Keep it away!" they both howled, kicking out at poor Scooby, who made more noise than ever.

"Keep what away?" asked Daphne innocently.

"That dog . . . that phantom dog!" shouted Dingle.

"Dog . . . what dog?" asked Granny Appleseed innocently. "I can't see any dog. Can you, girls?"

Velma and Daphne shook their heads again.

"It's there, pulling at my sleeve," insisted Wingle. "Surely you can all see it?"

The gang and Granny all shook their heads once more.

"You see, only rogues can see the phantom hound, as I said before," explained Freddie patiently. "And since you two can see it, there's obviously something on your consciences. Why don't you tell us about it . . .?"

"There's nothing to tell," snorted Wingle.

"Then the silver ghost dog will hound you forever," cried Daphne. "Just imagine, being chased by a dog for the rest of your lives!"

"Wingle, I can't stand it, I'll have to tell them," cried Dingle. "You see, old lady, we saw plans in the city architect's office. They want to build a block of modern apartments here and your cottage is in the middle of the site. They were going to offer you a good sum for the cottage and give you a rent free apartment with someone to act as janitor . . . with a garbage disposal unit, central heating . . ."

"And tap water?" cried Granny Appleseed, unable to believe her ears. "But that's really wonderful . . . something I've wanted all my life but never been able to afford, not even when my poor old Grandpa Joe was alive."

"And you two tried to trick an old widow woman out of a new home. Shame on you!" cried Daphne. "You deserve to be chased by the ghost dog for ever more."

"No, no, not that, we'll go away and never trouble you again," cried the two men, now thoroughly terrified at the thought.

And they shot out through the door and along the path, and disappeared up the road in a cloud of dust.

"Good old Scooby," cried the gang. "Well done!"

"Can you see Scooby noow?" wuffed Scooby, glad that the gang seemed willing to acknowledge him once more. "Scooby ughoo . . . this paint may be safe, but it tastes very nasty!"

"Come along, Scoob, I'll give you a bath," cried Shaggy.

"And then you shall have not one, but two bones, Scooby," promised Granny Appleseed. "Thanks to you, I shall soon have a new house!"

"I'll take the bones, but not the bath," howled Scooby. Oh, Scooby Doo, you'll never change, will you?

£ 2·50

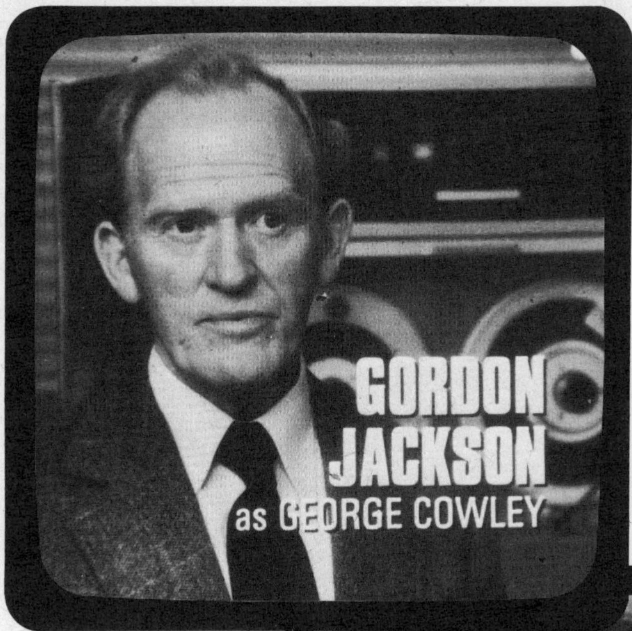
GORDON
JACKSON
as GEORGE COWLEY

MARTIN
SHAW
as DOYLE

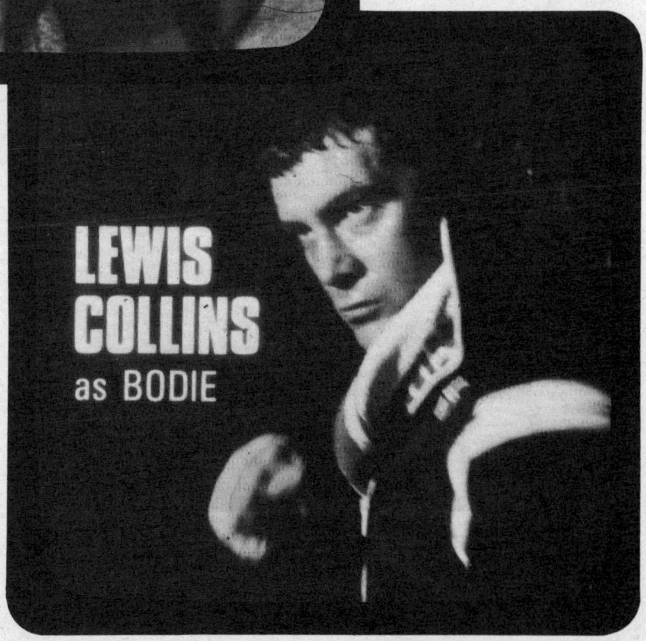
LEWIS
COLLINS
as BODIE

THE PROFESSIONALS
CI5

CI5

ANNUAL 1982

Published in Great Britain by Stafford Pemberton Publishing Ltd.,
The Ruskin Chambers, Drury Lane, Knutsford, Cheshire WA16 6HA.
Printed and bound in Italy
ISBN 0 86030 337 3

CONTENTS

Page	
8	Look Back with Gordon Jackson
12	Look Back with Martin Shaw
16	Look Back with Lewis Collins
20	When the Chips are Down
28	CI5 and the Man Behind It All
31	Win a Philips Video
32	Rest Cure
38	Faking a Fight
40	Word Search
41	Professionals Crossword
44	Lucky Break
48	Behind the Scenes
52	The One That Got Away
60	The Park — A Prize-Winning Poem
61	Action with Bodie and Doyle
62	The Embassy Incident
68	Stuntman in Action
72	Test of Strength

look back

with GORDON JACKSON

Here's the wee Gordon Jackson, a young Scot right down to his kilt! He's 11 or 12 years old and he's pictured on the bonnie banks of Loch Lomond — where else!

Here's Gordon on his very first day on his first film, on location in Cornwall in 1941. The film was "The Foreman Went to France". And his fellow actor? A young Tommy Trinder.

Another shot of Gordon in his family role as the young soldier, also taken in 1941 while making "The Foreman Went to France".

A very special day in Gordon's life — June 2nd, 1951, outside Chelsea Register Office where he married beautiful Scottish actress, Rona Anderson.

A recent photograph taken in the garden of his North London home with his two sons, Roddy on the left and Graham on the right. No wonder they've got film stars looks too!

LOOK BACK with GORDON..

Most actors perhaps like to think that they put their personal mark on each part they play, contributing something a little special from within themselves. Actor, Gordon Jackson, has given something very special to Major Cowley, head of CI5.

He gave exactly the same thing to the part of Hudson the much respected butler in the top TV series "Upstairs Downstairs", the part which made Gordon a household name after so many years of being the face we knew so well yet perhaps couldn't put a name to.

Can you guess what it was?

He gave them his very own Scottish accent!

"Neither Hudson nor Cowley were written as Scots" says Gordon, "but I was invited to play both parts and quite naturally played the part with a Scottish accent as I always do."

Gordon confesses that he finds it extremely difficult to speak without his accent and doesn't enjoy trying.

"I think you get away with an accent providing it's not too heavy and that the part doesn't specifically reveal that the person comes from a particular country or part of the country.

"I worked with Orson Welles and did an American play once. I told him I didn't think I could do an American accent. He told me it didn't matter — merely to give a suggestion of it, He said that if you played a part sincerely and fully, people wouldn't notice the accent and I think that's true."

It would be hard to imagine the tough-talking Cowley without his "dour Scot" identity now, wouldn't it?

The part itself is very typical of the characters which Gordon Jackson has been playing for many years — authoritarian, perhaps with the military or the law.

"I had not long finished filming 'Upstairs Downstairs' and had just done some live theatre when the script was offered to me," he says. "I don't know why they picked me. One of the producers, Albert Fennell, and I had worked together some years before on the film 'Tunes of Glory' so that might have had something to do with them thinking of me I suppose.

"I read the script and I liked it. I thought the part was right for me."

The part of Cowley was pretty clearly defined by Brian Clemens, the writer, and you could tell just what he wanted."

Brian Clemens agrees. He says "When I first conceived the series, I simply made Cowley a Northerner. It was a way of saying that I didn't see him as a public school boy, I wanted him to have a roughness factor.

"Of course, I didn't know who would be playing the parts when I first started to write it but when Gordon became Cowley, we simply adjusted the scripts."

If you met Gordon Jackson, however, you would soon realise just how much acting skill he has in portraying the ruthless hard man that Cowley is, for Gordon himself is a much gentler man who admits that acting is a compulsion he can't resist though he suffers agonies over learning his lines and never watches himself on the screen!

He originally comes from Glasgow where his father worked as a printer. He himself served a five year apprenticeship with Rolls-Royce there as a draughtsman.

Before he left school, however, his English teacher took him to the BBC drama department in Glasgow and his acting career started. He played parts on the radio.

He never saw himself as a star and it was only through someone else's recommendation that he was sought out and invited down to Ealing Studios where they were making propaganda films during the war.

Even then, he didn't look on the possibility of films as a career. He regarded his roles as the eternal Jock as his war effort!

Yet he has appeared in more than 50 movies, his parts growing with his experience.

He was in "Whisky Galore", "Tunes of Glory", "Mutiny on the Bounty", "The Ipcress File", "Those Magnificent Men in their Flying Machines", "The Medusa Touch" and "The Night of the Generals", to name but a few.

The film "Floodtide" back in 1949 was a very special one to him, however, for he met again a lovely young actress from Edinburgh called Rona Anderson who was playing the boss's daughter and he, the brilliant young ship designer.

Rona became his wife two years later and they now live in North London. Their two sons are Graham, who is 21, and Roddy, who is 19, neither of whom have followed in their parents' showbiz footsteps.

Despite the popular image of stars spending their time jet-setting around the world and dropping in at glittering parties nothing could be further from the truth in Gordon's case.

His first love is his home and his family and that's where he likes to spend his leisure time, apart from the odd trip to the sun, for he enjoys travelling.

He loves classical music, art and reading a good book — and that's where you'll often find him when he's not before the cameras — sitting quietly in a corner reading.

But don't get the impression that Gordon is some sort of introvert recluse! He loves being a part of the hive of activity that is filming, he loves being a part of the team, a part of the action and a part of the fun which inevitably threads its way among the constant bouts of hard slog.

look back with MARTIN SHAW

Some favourite photos from the Shaw family scrap-book, from tiny years to late teens. You will have read the stories behind the photographs in Martin's own story in this special 'Look Back' feature.

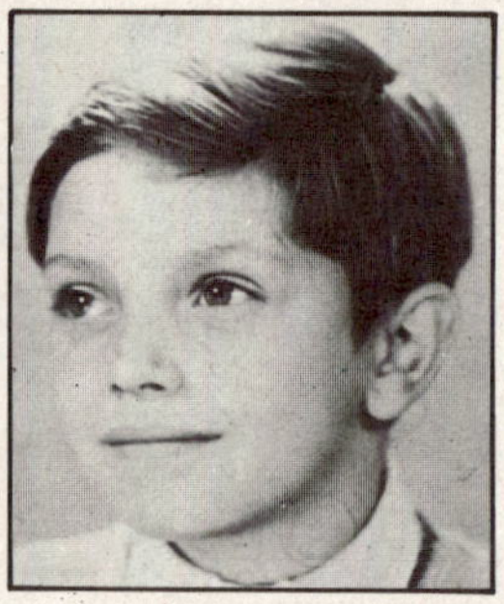

Although handsome actor, Martin Shaw, has built up a following of thousands of fans of all ages since he took on the role of Ray Doyle, he still steadfastly refuses to endorse any attempt to form an official fan club for him — "Fan clubs are for pop stars and personalities" he says, "not for actors."

But there is one special admirer in Martin's life and that's his number one fan, his mum, Mrs Jo Shaw. Mrs Shaw readily admits to being a proud and adoring mum. "When Martin was six weeks old, I had a photograph of him taken with me in my mother's garden. I thought he was the most wonderful thing that had ever happened to me in my life" she says.

"We're a very close family. No matter where Martin is, he rings us — even if he's in Australia or America."

"The photo with all four of us on was taken during a fabulous holiday on Bodmin Moor in Cornwall in a friend's cottage. Martin is twelve there and Jem is five years old.

"Jem was a little rogue. He was hilarious to be with and still is." But don't get excited, girls, Martin's younger brother is married with two children of his own now.

"They have never seen Martin in 'The Professionals' though," says Mrs Shaw. "It's on too late at night for them. One of them goes to school and the other children tell him about the programme."

The family lived with Mrs Shaw's parents when Martin was young. "It was just after the war and you couldn't get houses," remembers Mrs Shaw. Despite the fact that money was tight, though, the family did have some super holidays and over the page, you'll find photos from their family scrapbook.

"Martin was only four-and-a-half when we went to Golden Sands at Rhyl," says Mrs Shaw. "We stayed in a caravan because we couldn't afford anything more expensive. You'll notice he doesn't look very happy on the picture of the three of us riding the bicycle. That's because he wanted to drive himself!"

LOOK BACK with MARTIN..

It was Martin's mum and his dad, Frank, who gave him his first taste of showbiz when he was a little boy. They both took part in amateur dramatics and Mrs Shaw's mum, the late Mrs Agnes Eastwood, used to sing as well.

Mr and Mrs Shaw did a song and dance act too and it wasn't long before Martin got roped in. "I can clearly remember my first steps onto a stage. I wore a straw boater and glasses and held a carrier bag. I had to say hello to the audience and make the pipe drop into the carrier bag. Not bad for a three-year-old!" says Martin.

The audience loved it. The trouble was I hadn't learned about entrances and exits and my Dad had to carry me off!"

Another time when the family all got in on the act was at a street party in fancy dress. Dad was Al Jolson, Nanny Eastwood was Al's Mammy and Martin took off Arthur English's then famous "Spiv" act, offering nylons for sale to the girls! All three won first prize in their sections.

Martin has another faithful fan in his grandmother, Nanny Alice Hatfield, who keeps the photograph of Martin taken at L.A.M.D.A. when he was nineteen (pictured over page) on her sideboard. "She says she likes that photograph because the insurance man recognised Martin when he called at her home" says Mrs Shaw. "She's in her eighties now but she's a real fan of Martin's. Martin went to visit her recently and her home help Grace Cox was there. Grace nearly fainted when she saw Martin walk in through Nanny's door."

Martin himself is grateful to his father, Frank, for encouraging many of his interests. "It is his knowledge and interest in such a wide range of subjects from astrology to zoology which has given me a lot of material and knowledge to draw on as a mature person" says Martin.

Another photo from the album shows Martin, in short trousers and ankle socks, sitting next to his mother on a park bench. "I can't remember where it was taken," says Mrs Shaw, "but I can remember the day afterwards, he came out with measles!"

An old school portrait brings back a smile to Mrs Shaw's face but it doesn't bring back happy memories for Martin. "Martin hated school" she says. "At that time he just wasn't intellectually inclined, even though he had passed his 11-plus and was in the grammar school stream.

"From being fourteen he just wanted to be an actor. He was in all the school plays. He is very one-pointed about anything he does and he wasn't interested in anything but acting."

It was Tom Knowles, a teacher at Martin's school who nurtured Martin's talent and after schooldays were over, Martin joined Tom's semi-pro drama group, the Pied Piper Players. They did improvised street theatre, knocking on doors and inviting people onto a bombsite where they performed!

Eventually, he got a place at L.A.M.D.A. — the London Academy of Music and Dramatic Arts. "They gave me everything I needed to know" says Martin. "I developed a real 'gut' feeling for acting there. I was taught to be a chameleon — to change both the body and the mind according to the part."

He was top student of his year and was lucky enough to be offered a job straight from college at the Hornchurch Repertory Company. "I was taken on as Assistant Stage Manager which meant I did everything. I'd hang scenery, sweep the stage, make the tea and still have to learn six parts. But I loved it."

After a brief spell with the Bristol Old Vic, he was 'discovered' by the television media and was offered some first rate parts. In 1968, he played Cliff in "Look Back in Anger" at the Royal Court Theatre with Jane Asher.

He played the drunken Dr Evans in the televised "Doctor in the House" series, one of the four TV series he has made. And he played Horatio in the transatlantic production of "Hamlet" with Sir John Gielgud, Richard Chamberlain and Michael Redgrave. He's made three films and been nominated for awards for two of them, Polanski's "Macbeth" and "Operation Daybreak" (televised early in 1981 on the same night as a "Professionals" episode — a rare treat for Martin's fans).

"When I got Marlon Brando's role in "A Streetcar Named Desire" he confesses, "I used to drive round Picadilly Circus just staring at my name in big neon lights! But it was also a bit scary because I thought, 'Now that I've gained that sort of stature, I'll have to make sure I deserve it'."

Now that filming "The Professionals" series is over, there is little doubt that Martin Shaw will continue to be offered superb parts to play. "My career doesn't begin and end with Ray Doyle" he says. And while Doyle fans know that eventually, he will disappear from the small screen, they can be sure that the name of Martin Shaw will be around for a lot longer.

look back

with LEWIS COLLINS

Little Lew, aged two and a half years old

A happy family group. Lew, aged eight, with his mother, Jane and his father, Bill, and sister, Valerie.

Lew's extra proud cos his is a racing bike with those dropped-handle bars that all boys love to have.

His claim to pop fame — The Mojos. Now which one would you say is Lew?

Lew wears a treasured possession — a leather jacket given to him by Paul McCartney.

The handsome, debonair and really smooth Gavin, the part which brought Lew big success in "The Cuckoo Waltz".

Here's Lew and Bill, his father, snapped on holiday. Note the moustache.

LOOK BACK with LEWIS . .

He's tall. He's dark. He's handsome and he's a real live action man with an impressive list of hobbies and sporting activities which gave him tailor-made training for the part of tough CI5 agent, Bodie.

Lewis Collins started life in the tough dockside area of Birkenhead, Liverpool, where his father, Bill, worked as a shipwright. He was born on May 27, 1946, his sister, Valerie's fifth birthday and a couple of weeks after his brother, Gerald had had his tenth birthday.

Although he was the baby of the family, Lew stood on his own two feet and fought his own battles in his days at Bidston Primary School and Grange School.

"I found you had to know how to look after yourself where I came from," he says, "the kids didn't just fight with their fists — they would use anything that came to hand."

Even so, he looks back on his childhood as a happy time, full of fun and adventure. And little wonder for the Collins family liked the open-air life with camping holidays and hill-walking.

Lewis developed an interest in guns and target-shooting whilst helping out on his aunt's farm in Shropshire and at 12 years old, he joined the Liverpool Central Rifle Club at Mason Street Barracks to take part in .22 calibre league matches .303 service-rifle shooting on the Army's Altcar Rifle Ranges near Liverpool. He won competitions and trophies.

On the rough tracks and roads at Altcar, Lew also learned to drive and to ride motor cycles, all good basic training for a much tougher assignment he set himself later in life when he took up parachuting as a hobby three years ago.

Breaking an ankle during training didn't make him the most popular guy around, however, for it brought filming of the second series of "The Professionals" to a halt. He did, however, join the Parachute Regiment of the Territorial Army Volunteer Reserve and spent ten months building up physically for the Acceptance Course. He ran miles in army boots and webbing loaded with sand as a dead weight — up to 80lbs at a time!

Sounds gruelling but Lew enjoyed it.

"That's my idea of having a good time," he says. "There's nothing I find more relaxing than a good work out."

And at the same time, he finished off the second series of "The Professionals" and filmed the third!

A year ago, he got through the final selection course and earned his Red Beret.

It's perhaps not easy to imagine someone with such a tough image being keen on playing the piano and taking part in Shakespearean productions but Lew is, after all, born under the sign of the twins, Gemini, and typical of the sign, has many facets to his character.

His father, a local dance band leader in his spare time, played the piano to him when he was only an hour old and later, Lew managed a few songs on the old Joanna himself but found his real talent musically when he was thirteen. He learned to play drums and he and his father, a pianist, played the clubs together at weekends for over three years.

Lew also joined a rock 'n' roll band at 13 called The Renegades and within a couple of years, they were playing at the famous Cavern Club in Liverpool, sometimes on the same night as those famous Beatles.

"He and Colin, his cousin, were a pair of comics," says his father in a biography he has written for members of Lew's fan club, the Friendship Circle.

"Colin was a quitarist and sometimes they played and sang in the same group. They were a couple of rough and ready lads but much loved and were considered notorious by the locals.

"They have been inseparable mates ever since. Lew was Colin's best man and one day, no doubt, the situation will be reversed."

Too young to become a fully professional musician when he left school at 15, Lew decided to develop yet another artistic facet to his nature and became a ladies hair stylist at Andre Bernard's salon in Liverpool.

Mike McCartney, Paul's brother, worked there too and they became friends. Lew got his first taste for acting through working on new sketches for Mike's satirical group "The Scaffold".

But still, Lew wasn't happy with the way his life was going so he learned to play a guitar, turned pro, and ended up with The Mojos.

They had had one hit and went on to score another three in the next couple of years. After their break-up in '66, he spent eight months with the Rob Storme Group, and six months with a re-formed Mojos, but when that group ended, so did Lew's career as a musician.

"He had to think deeply about his life once again," says his father, "and, to fill in time, he took one ordinary job after another.

"He became a lorry driver, a clothes salesman, a van delivery man, a waiter. One day, whilst on his latest job — a door to door salesman selling lemonade and crisps — he pulled into a lay-by, leaned heavily on the steering wheel and said to himself, 'What am I doing here?' Then it all became crystal clear. 'I'm sure I could act' he thought 'on the legitimate stage . . . do it properly . . .' And from then on he knew where he was going."

He trained at the London Academy of Music and Dramatic Art for three years and then on to Chesterfield Repertory Company for a year as an actor-assistant stage manager, which means when you haven't got a part in a production you have to help with all the back-stage jobs.

"It was gruelling," he says, "but well worth it. I got my Equity card and learnt the ropes."

A varied career followed and he made his way up the acting ladder until he was in the West End theatre and getting small TV parts too.

He appeared in series like "Warship", "Z-Cars", "Crown Court", "Rooms", "Marked Personal" and "The New Avengers".

It was in 1974 that he played Bobby, the lead in "They Disappear When You Lie Down", which won him the part of Gavin in "The Cuckoo Waltz" which ran to three series between 1974 and 1976.

It was an episode in "The New Avengers", however, entitled "Obsession" that led to him being cast as Bodie. He played a tough ex-mercenary soldier — a much different character to the smoothy Gavin.

Between filming the four series of Professionals programmes he has managed to fit in other TV engagements, his hectic keepfit training for the paras, personal appearances, and fan club dates.

If you want details of Lew's Friendship Circle, send an s.a.e. to Chris Wassell, at 160, Thirlmere Gardens, Northwood, Middlesex.

When the chips are down

Rakshash and Stoller drive off...
Followed closely by Bodie and Doyle...
YOU THINK THEY'LL MAKE THE DEAL TONIGHT?
I DOUBT IT. THESE GUYS ARE BIG BUSINESS. IT TAKES TIME TO SET UP THEIR KIND OF DEALS.
Suddenly Stoller's car, lights switched off, pulls alongside...
HEY MATE!
UNH?
PRESENT FOR YOU — FROM THE BOSS.
As precious seconds tick by...
IT'S ROLLED UNDER THE SEAT! WE'LL HAVE TO—
JUMP!
KA-ROOM

YOU ALL RIGHT MATE ?
NO THANKS TO YOU, BUTTERFINGERS.
That morning, in Cowley's office.
IT SEEMS EMIL'S BEEN SEEN TALKING TO EX-PRESIDENT N'GANA IN PARIS.
YOU RECKON N'GANA'S PLANNING A COMEBACK ?
MAYBE. HIS COUNTRY'S IN TURMOIL AND SOME NEW EQUIPMENT COULD GIVE HIM ENOUGH MUSCLE TO GET BACK IN POWER.
SO HE ASKS EMIL RAKSHASH TO GET IT FOR HIM.
AND EMIL SETS UP A DEAL WITH STOLLER FOR THE WEAPONS.
THAT'S RIGHT. AND AS YOU TWO KNOW RUDY STOLLER IS AN EXTREMELY CAREFUL MAN.
TOO RIGHT, BOSS.
DRING DRING
The phone interrupts their speculation....
COWLEY HERE... YES... YES... ALL RIGHT WE'LL BE OVER THERE IN TEN MINUTES.
THEY'VE FOUND A BODY IN A DERELICT HOUSE OFF THE PORTOBELLO ROAD... IT'S DESCRIPTION WOULD SEEM TO FIT EMIL RAKSHASH.

Minutes later....
IT'S RAKSHASH ALL RIGHT. HE MUST HAVE GOT STOLLER ANGRY
A ROLL OF TWENTIES? WHAT FOR?
THIS WAS FOUND STUFFED IN HIS MOUTH...
Cowley's expert eye spots something unusual...
THEY'RE COUNTERFEIT...THEY'RE GOOD... VERY GOOD — BUT FAKE.
YOU MEAN RAKSHASH MADE A DOWN PAYMENT WITH FUNNY MONEY, STOLLER SPOTTED IT AND KILLED HIM?
LOOKS LIKE IT, BUT WHY? RAKSHASH WOULD HAVE MADE ENOUGH ON THIS DEAL WITHOUT TRYING TO RIP STOLLER OFF.
YOU'RE RIGHT— IT DOESN'T MAKE SENSE. WHY WOULD RAKSHASH JEOPARDISE THE DEAL BEFORE IT GOT OFF THE GROUND?
SO WE'VE GOT A MYSTERY— WHAT DO WE DO?
YOU TWO WATCH THE EXCELSIOR HOTEL.
ONE OF N'GANA'S AIDES IS STAYING THERE. IF STOLLER STILL WANTS TO DO BUSINESS HE'LL CONTACT HIM.

HIS NAMES ELAZAAN. YOU CAN PICK UP HIS FILE AT THE OFFICE.
WHAT ARE YOU GOING TO DO SIR?
I DON'T KNOW... MAYBE I'LL BRUSH UP MY RUSSIAN ACCENT...
!?
Outside the Excelsior . . .
THAT'S HIM.
EXCELSIOR HOTEL
AND THAT GORILLA WITH HIM IS ONE OF STOLLER'S GOONS.
This time, Bodie and Doyle wait..
THERE GOES THE COVER.
TAIL THEM.
They drive to a large warehouse.
YOU THINK THEY'VE GOT THE STUFF IN THERE?
THERE'S ONE WAY TO FIND OUT.
The two men make for the roof...
And . . .

WE'LL TAKE THEM ONE BY ONE. THESE PAPERS WILL ALLOW US TO DRIVE STRAIGHT ONTO THE SHIP.
IT'S A PLEASURE DOING BUSINESS WITH YOU. THE PRESIDENT WILL BE PLEASED.
YOU STAY HERE WITH MOOSE. WE'LL BE BACK FOR THE OTHER CONTAINERS.
THE FINAL PAYMENTS WILL BE MADE ABOARD SHIP.
THEY'RE GOING — COME ON.
As the truck leaves . . .
OOF!
As the truck heads for the docks, Bodie and Doyle make their way forward.
Inside the cab . . .
WHAT EXACTLY HAVE WE GOT IN THE BACK, BOSS?
GOOD OLD AMERICAN FIREPOWER ... THE BEST IN THE WORLD!

Suddenly . . .
STOP THIS TRUCK!
UNH? WHA-?
NO WAY— BLAST HIM!
But . . .
BOOM!
TOO LATE, PAL!
Stoller is wounded . . .
GET OFF THIS CRATE! IT'S GOING TO CRASH!
Bodie and Doyle jump free . . .
GARAGE CLOSED
CRRUNCH!
UUURGH . . . OH NO!
PETROL
TROL
KER-ASH

B-DOOMPH
Later, after Moose and Elazaan have been rounded up . . .
WELL, THAT'S ONE LITTLE WAR WE'VE MANAGED TO PREVENT. WELL DONE.
THANKS BOSS. BY THE WAY, HOW DID YOU GET ON?
I WENT TO EL MAMBO'S FOR A LITTLE FLUTTER. I CLOSED THE PLACE DOWN.
YOU MEAN YOU BROKE THE BANK?
I HAD THE OWNERS ARRESTED. THEY'D BEEN WORKING A NICE LITTLE SCHEME TO UNLOAD COUNTERFEIT MONEY.
YOU MEAN THAT'S WHERE RAKSHASH GOT HIS MONEY? HE DIDN'T KNOW IT WAS COUNTERFEIT?
APPARENTLY NOT. IF A BIG SPENDING FOREIGNER WINS AT EL MAMBO'S HE IS PAID OUT IN FALSE NOTES. IT WAS RAKSHASH'S MISFORTUNE THAT STOLLER FOUND OUT THE NOTES WERE FAKE.
I SIMPLY ADOPTED A THICK RUSSIAN ACCENT, THEN ALL I HAD TO DO WAS WIN. SURE ENOUGH THEY PAID ME WITH COUNTERFEIT MONEY.
I'VE GOT A QUESTION, BOSS.
YES, DOYLE — WHAT IS IT?
HOW ABOUT LETTING US TWO KNOW YOUR SYSTEM?
I'LL DRINK TO THAT.

CI5 AND THE MAN BEHIND IT ALL ....

If you ever stop to wonder where the idea for "The Professionals" series came from you might start to conjure up visions of a writer glancing at a newspaper headline one morning on the train and suddenly being inspired to write about two daring heroes who rescued the hostages and brought the villains to justice.

We often read, don't we, about authors who get a brilliant idea seemingly out of thin air and turn it into a top rate novel, film or TV series? And if that was the story behind the birth of CI5 then it would seem a suitably romantic and exciting one.

The true facts, however, are much more mundane and yet perhaps they highlight even more the remarkable talent of the writer who created the series, Brian Clemens.

"I simply went to London Weekend Television and asked them what sort of material they were looking for at that particular time. They told me they would be interested in seeing my ideas for a fast-moving adventure series on crime-fighting centred around two main characters.

"I produced two themes, one about two undercover policemen and one about two CI5 agents. They chose CI5."

It was in February, 1977, that Brian first put pen to paper on the series which was to turn into a whole host of exciting episodes filmed as four series of programmes, the last of which is currently being screened.

His own original name for the programme was "The A Squad" — "but that was only what we call a working title" says Brian — and before the first episode burst onto the TV screen it had become "The Professionals".

It's hard to visualise anyone else but Gordon Jackson, Martin Shaw and Lewis Collins in the three major roles and yet as the writer of the series, Brian had no idea who would be playing the roles of Cowley, Doyle and Bodie.

His job was to set about creating the central characters. But how does a writer do that?

"The basis of any duo relationship is that it has to have an element of conflict. You would end up with a very dull 'marriage' if the characters liked each other all the time. There is no drama unless there is some conflict.

"Let's say you have a story about a man under seige in a house and Bodie and Doyle say 'Come out!' and he does then you've got no story, have you?

"You can't have them kicking doors in all the time. There has to be parts where they are simply going from A to B and on the way, they have to have something to talk about. They might, for instance, be investigating a crime about aquariums and one of them will say that he used to keep goldfish when he was younger. The other one will probably say that the only way he likes fish is with batter round it!

"The way I saw it was that Bodie was a swine and Doyle was the one with the conscience."

This was how Brian in fact described the two in his original notes for LWT:

"Ray Doyle is nearly 30. Doyle? Well, maybe way back there is a touch of the Gaelic about him (and that would explain two aspects of his character) but he certainly doesn't look it; his hair is fair, his eyes are blue and his handsome face has a deceptively gentle look to it. It's those blue eyes really, they have a lazy, dreamy way of looking at you. Just before he hits you! In the girl/bed stakes, his eyes are his biggest ammunition. Nor does he sound Gaelic — Ray's a Londoner, not a Bow Bell's Cockney, South of the river. But on a clear day, with the wind in the right direction, he might just have heard them."

(If you're a Martin Shaw fan, you already have said to yourself 'But Martin has green eyes, not blue!' OK. So the colour of his eyes didn't fit Brian Clemens' initial concept of Doyle, but you've to admit, everything else fits!)

"Ray's a copper. Detective, CID. Mind you, he didn't start out for the police; no, he worked in a shop and studied art in the evenings (his stories about those nude models often enlive a stake-out!) — then he realised he had no talent, except for appreciation. So he joined the force.

"He was out of uniform and into CID plain clothes in record time — because of that special 'way' he has with him, that deceptively gentle way. Some tough postings around the East End, then into the Yard proper on special duties. He's the finest shot with a handgun in the entire Met Division.

"Those touches of Gaelic? Well, he can be a bit of a dreamer, an idealist, verging on the romantic; funny the job hasn't knocked it out of him, but it hasn't. And, Gaelic style, side by side with the dreamer is a terrible temper. Oh, it takes something huge to arouse it — but when he does flare . . . . !

"Girls? Well, a man who looks like that, girls would have to figure in his life, wouldn't they? Two have to the point of getting engaged (both gave the ring back and he wears it on a chain under his shirt). The job and permanent relationships don't mix so now he plays the field. And he works for CI5 and if anyone in that amoral organisation has leanings towards morality, it's Ray Doyle."

So that was how Brian Clemens saw Doyle. What about Bodie?

He wrote "William Andrew Philip Bodie. But he answers only to Bodie. He's maybe two years younger than Ray, though you'd never know it. In fact, you might take him for older than Ray. See him downing a pint in a Kings Road Club and you might mistake him for a Chelsea player. Certainly he has the powerful, pugnacious build of a goal scorer; and the confidence of a man who *knows* he can handle himself. From his dark hair to his balanced stance, he exudes the kind of aggression that seems to go hand in hand with success these days. He likes to dress well too — not a dandy, but he takes care over his appearance.

"Bodie's a soldier, Sergeant. 19th Airborne. Bodie's formative years are open to conjecture because each time he tells it, it gets bigger! Certainly he joined the Merchant Navy when he was 17. Certainly he jumped ship in East Africa and joined a mercenary force. Probably he lived with — and off — an older woman in Cape Town. Undeniably he joined HM Forces when he was 23.

"It is a matter of record that he served in Northern Ireland at the height of the troubles, and a matter of conjecture that he took part in several undocumented raids in Jordan.

"His particular skills are rifle shooting and climbing. His hobbies are rifle shooting, climbing and girls. Usually girls who are socially above him but that doesn't concern Bodie, give him an audience and he's away. If Ray is a romantic, Bodie is a romancer (except that there is usually more than a grain of truth in his stories).

"If CI5 is amoral, then Bodie is its star turn. The job is all that matters, and if people get in the way, then hard luck. He's not a bigot per se but the word 'wog' still crops up in his vocabulary and he's apt to call a spade a spade — and end up fighting a room full of them!"

Brian Clemens hands the credit for teaming Bodie and Doyle together to Cowley. "It was Cowley's little stroke of genius, his incisive knowledge of human nature . . . because Ray and Bodie are the blade and the steel, the flint and the wheel, each complementary and indispensable to the other."

His ideas for Cowley as the tough wardog who has had his active service curtailed by injury and who now finds himself forced to take a back seat to the Bodies and Doyles of the service have seen a couple of changes as the series has progressed.

Brian first saw Cowley with a "bur of Northern accent" but when Scottish actor, Gordon Jackson, was cast in the role, it became a very Northern accent — a real Scot in fact.

But perhaps a bigger change has been the work of the programmes' producers who have gradually seen Cowley as a more active man than Brian first envisaged him.

He gave him a limp "I wanted him to be an erascable man. That sort of thing comes out of being a man of action, shot in the leg and chairborne. He would like to be out with the boys." Current producers have played that back a bit.

Cowley is still the sort of commander Brian envisaged however — a unique personality.

"Cowley — sometimes affectionately and safely out of his earshot, referred to as 'The Cow' — was for some years MI5's most unpopular and ultimately most respected administrator.

"Joining MI5, in the wake of the Philby and Blake debacles. Cowley was quick to realise that MI5 was hopelessly outmoded in concept. It didn't stand a prayer against the sheer professionalism of security forces in Israel, South Africa, France, Germany or Russia; the age of the talented amateur, the time of the Oxford Don asked to 'keep an eye out while you're doing that dig in Syria, old chap' was over.

"Cowley realised that 'who you know' had to be replaced by 'know how', and he set about it, weeding out the languid dross and replacing them with tough, hard men to deal with new tough, hard situations. At first, Cowley's burr of Northern accent was a positive demerit; but it soon became associated with very plain speaking indeed. And getting the job done. Even his jealous rivals had to admit that "I don't like the man but if I'm going to be sent to risk my neck, I'd rather *he* set up the job!"

It took Brian Clemens two weeks to write the first script. "The writing doesn't take long but it takes a lot of thinking time" he says. "In the first script, you are setting down the basic principles and rules that then have to be obeyed. You are stuck with it from then on.

"You might think it quite interesting, for instance, to have the head of the bureau with a stutter and it would make one very funny episode. But after 56 episodes, it gets very boring. You have to be very careful about what characteristics you give them, which areas they live and even what sort of home they live in. Decisions taken at that time had to last me through five years of the series."

Apart from establishing the three major characters and developing the relationships between them, Brian had to set this against a background of action-packed TV drama.

The brief he laid down at that time was that any political motivations must be subjegated to the ordinary human involvement; situations could be stolen from the headlines and no situation must suspend belief. He knew it had to keep moving and fast. The idea was to set up the story, set up the problem CI5 have to deal with and then let the audience see how they solve the apparently insoluble, all the time keeping the relationship of Ray and Bodie — with Cowley — firmly in the foreground.

Just as Cowley, Doyle and Bodie have become so real to viewers through the talents of the star actors, so many young fans firmly believe that CI5 is a *real* Government department, perhaps because Brian Clemens' original concept of such a squad seems on the face of it to be such a valid idea.

But even if there is such a squad operating in this country to-day, certainly Brian's CI5 is not based on any leak of top secret info in his direction! He conceived CI5 in the same way as he 'manufactured Doyle and Bodie' — to fit LWT's brief.

He set its inception back in 1971 as an answer to the increased trend towards violence which was causing concern in high circles.

"In November, 1971, a meeting was called by the Home Secretary; also present were prominent members of the Police and the Armed Forces; while MI5 was represented by George Cowley.

"The subject under discussion was the increased use of violence, coercion techniques and sophisticated weapons in this country; a trend spearheaded by terrorist movements, but rapidly emulated by criminal factions.

"Cases were cited of hi-jackings, bomb threats hostage kidnappings and snipers — all representing a threat not only to law and order in Great Britain but also to the general populace.

"One point became clear; often the antagonist was better organised than the authority that had to combat him; often the police had to request specialised services of the military (and vice versa); frequently these demarcations and divisions of responsibility resulted in confusion and dangerous delays.

"The meeting came to one important decision; to form some very special men into a very special squad, with a very special brief:

1. to elevate criminal intelligence to the very sophisticated levels already existing in military intelligence and thus attempt to defuse these situations before they had a chance to escalate.
2. To deal with these situations if or when they did get out of hand.

"Thus CI5 — Criminal Intelligence 5."

Brian saw CI5 as no more than forty men, specialists from all the forces available — Commandos, SAS, Marines, Paras, Police and, although it could never be admitted, at least two men drawn from the wrong side of the law including a safe cracker who served 11 years on the Moor.

They work from a small suite of offices actually within the Home Office with 'Home Affairs (S)' on the door. S is for Security.

The sort of jobs they tackle can start small — some kids, waste land, an empty ammunition box — and quickly escalate to a square mile of the city, and you know that somewhere there is a sniper. Where is he? Who is his target?

Or the arrested terrorist — and the innocent hostage snatched and held in retaliation — to be exchanged.

The joy-riders who steal a car, not knowing about the powerful bomb in the boot. And all the while they are driving deeper into congested areas.

Panic used as a weapon to extort money — to pay up or I'll explode a device in the stadium and start a human stampede.

These are all themes we have seen on our screens along with so many more, all the while building up our knowledge and understanding of the work of CI5 yet each week thrilled and mystified by the never-ending fascination of it all. And the good thing is that there are still more exciting episodes 'in the can' and yet to be seen.

For the professional behind The Professionals, however, there are new challenges to face and Brian Clemens is hard at work creating new dramas for the screen.

WIN A PHILIPS VIDEO IN OUR FREE COMPETITION

WORTH OVER £600

How would you like to be able to watch your favourite TV programme "The Professionals" whenever you want to — just to switch on and tune in to Bodie and Doyle, Cowley and the adventures of CI5, re-living your favourite episodes over and over again?

The answer, of course, is to get yourself a Video Cassette Recorder. Now how would you like one of the latest Videos ABSOLUTELY FREE OF CHARGE?

All you have to do is to enter our free competition and you could be the lucky winner of **PHILIPS NEW REVOLUTIONARY VIDEO RECORDING SYSTEM, the VR2020**.

Look at these superb features: *The* VR2020, the first in Philips VIDEO 2000 series, is the first video system with a flip-over cassette. That means you get twice as much playing time — up to EIGHT hours — because you record on both sides of the tape.

Apart from recording your favourite programme as you watch it so that you can see it over and over again, you can even record it while you're away on holiday! You can set your video up to 16 days ahead. And, of course, you can record one side while you watch a programme on the other channel.

Dynamic Track Following to ensure a perfect picture every playback.

Micro-processor Control which even helps you plan your programmes — and won't let you make mistakes!

Special "Go To" button which enables you to get to an exact point on the cassette automatically — and quickly.

Dynamic Noise Suppression to improve sound quality by suppressing noise in both the recording and playback modes.

Modular Construction for easy servicing.

WHAT MORE COULD YOU ASK?

HOW TO ENTER

Here's how to enter: Answer the three questions below and then fill in the tie-breaker. Send your answer on a POSTCARD to:
102, London Road, Apsley, Hemel Hempstead, Herts.
by January 31st, 1982. Mark your entry "Video".

Question 1: What are Bodie's two middle names?

Question 2: Was Doyle formerly with MI5, CID or SAS?

Question 3: Is Cowley a Chief Superintendent, a Major or a Captain?

VCR and CI5 MAKE A GOOD TEAM BECAUSE ....
(not more than 20 words).

REST CURE

A buzzer sounded on the secretary's desk and she got up and opened the door. Bodie and Doyle walked in.

"What is it this time chief?" asked Bodie. Cowley finished shuffling some papers and looked up.

"You've been working very hard lately, haven't you?" he said.

"That's the way we like it," said Doyle.

"That's the way I like it too, Doyle, but your escapade at the tractor exhibition seems to have ruffled a lot of feathers."

"But sir," cried Doyle indignantly, "you know that half the 'agricultural advisers' at the exhibition were agents, and that Mengel was playing them off against each other. If we hadn't acted someone would have got killed!"

"That may be so," agreed Cowley quietly, "but a lot of important people thought that blowing the place up was a little too drastic."

"We caught Mengel and Frieman," Bodie pointed out.

"Yes, but it was all too public. You were lucky not to have your pictures all over the papers. Anyway —" Cowley looked from Bodie to Doyle, "— the two of you are taking a holiday. I don't want to see you for two weeks. The rest will do you good."

"But sir —" protested Doyle.

"You will do as you're told," said Cowley with finality. "Now get out of here."

Bodie and Doyle walked out of the building and into the streets. They made their way through the busy crowds of shoppers thronging the sunny pavements. They had reached the broad esplanade of the Thames Embankment before Bodie spoke.

"What do you think, mate?" he asked.

"It's wrong," replied Bodie, his fingers flexing nervously at his sides, his eyes roaming to and fro, scanning the crowds. "The whole thing's just wrong. Cowley shouldn't give in to pressure like that. I can't just switch off. I keep getting the uneasy feeling that something's suddenly going . . ."

Doyle's words were interrupted by a woman's shrill scream. "'Ere you, come back with that. Stop. Somebody stop him." The two men looked up and saw a small bespectacled man running across the open terrace towards them clutching a woman's handbag. The owner of the handbag, a curly blonde in red tank top and jeans, was in hot pursuit. Doyle reacted instantly to the woman's cries and as the fugitive approached a blow from his stiffened forearm sent him stumbling to the floor. "You've got a blinkin' nerve," said the girl breathlessly to the fallen thief, retrieving her stolen bag and beginning to belabour him with it.

"Please don't," he pleaded, raising an arm to protect himself and fumbling for his glasses, "I didn't want to do it, I was forced to." "They made me."

"Alright, who made you?" asked Doyle, helping the man ward off the blows from the girl's handbag.

"They made me. They told me to take her handbag and run for the car over there." But there was no car in the place that the man indicated, only an empty space at the kerbside.

Suddenly, in a confused flurry of activity from further down the Embankment, a woman screamed, a figure was bundled into the back of a car, the car door slammed and tyres screeched across the pavement. "There," said the man, pointing excitedly, "that's them." By this time the limousine was already disappearing into the stream of fast flowing traffic.

"All right," said Bodie grasping the smaller man's collar and lifting him up on tip toe, "why don't you tell us what this is all about? Start with your name and the names of whoever was in that car."

"My name is Arnold Pebblewhite," said the man timidly, "I work as a clerk in a city insurance office. The work, though easy, is less than demanding. However, in my private life I have a weakness. A weakness that has led me into troubled waters before, though never, I hasten to add, into anything as serious as this. I love to gamble, you see, and in the car I pointed out were two gentlemen to whom I owed a debt."

"What were their names?"

"Charles and Maxwell Kinross. They own the Blue Cockatoo gaming rooms in South London. I'm afraid in my weakness I ran up a debt there I could never pay. Maxwell wanted to break my leg but Charles offered me an alternative. He said the debt would be forgotten if I were to snatch this lady's bag."

"Why?"

"The object of the exercise was not simply to secure Miss Moorhouse's bag. This was simply a ruse to lure her to the waiting car."

The girl, having checked the contents of her bag, snapped it shut and once more struck Arnold Pebblewhite with it. "You must be barmy Mister Pigglewick if you think . . ."

"My name is Pebblewhite," corrected the clerk, "many people have trouble remembering it."

"Not half as much as you're having remembering mine," she said, striking him again, "Miss blinking Moorhouse. My name's Angela Babcock and I'm here on a mini weekend holiday from Leeds."

Although still cowering from the rain of blows Pebblewhite looked surprised. Bodie turned to Doyle. "You know what's happened, don't you?"

Doyle nodded. "Mistaken identity. All we have to do is find someone who looks like Angela Babcock."

"There was someone," said the girl from Yorkshire, "I noticed her when we were being shown round the old galleon on the quayside. She was wearing jeans and a similar red top to mine. She was about the same age and height as well. When I last saw her she was standing on her own, over there," she pointed to the empty stretch of the Embankment where a minute or so earlier they had watched the hurried departure of the Kinross brothers' car. "That was just before I was attacked by Mister Pebbledash."

But Bodie was listening no longer. Already he was hailing a taxi.

* * * * * * * * *

It took them longer than they had expected to find the Blue Cockatoo and after the sunlit bustle of the streets the deserted, neonlit interior was quiet and cool as a subterranean cave. The card and roulette tables were closed. Bodie heard voices murmuring. He peered across the mock leather and brass at two men talking in a corner booth. "The Kinross brothers," he murmured to Doyle.

"Sorry gents," said one of the men, "We're closed." When neither Bodie nor Doyle replied he repeated the statement.

"We're looking for someone."

"We're a gaming club, not a missing persons bureau."

"Her name's Moorhouse," said Bodie and watched for the reaction his remarks made. When one of the brothers moved his hands from view Bodie grasped the man's hair and brought his face forward until it was in contact with the tabletop. Doyle drew his gun. "Now tell us where she is."

"Who are you guys?" muttered the man from his prone position.

"Bad news for the likes of you. Where is she?"

When there was no reply to his partner's question Doyle loosened the safety catch on his gun. "Okay, I'm convinced," said the taller of the two brothers who still sat upright. "The girl's not here. The contract simply said to snatch her and deliver her to the Tower Bridge as soon as we'd done so. There a guy takes delivery and pays us off."

"Who was the guy and where did he take her?"

Kinross shrugged. "He's an American named Wilbur Jamieson. Why he wants the girl or where he's taken her I couldn't tell you. That's all I know."

"Dead end," said Bodie angrily. "How can we find a guy in London with nothing to go on but a name and nationality?"

Doyle thought for a moment and then grinned. "I'll ask Mr. Cow," he said, and walked across to the payphone in the foyer. Bodie watched him speak urgently into the mouthpiece. He returned grinning in a few moments. "It's all fixed. Cowley's going to get back to us. We might as well lock these two meatheads in the broom cupboard while we're waiting."

Then minutes later the phone rang and Doyle hurried to answer it. He listened a moment and then replaced the receiver. "Jamieson's at the Parkway Hotel. Let's go and get him."

* * * * * * * * *

"How did you get Cowley to come up with his whereabouts?" Bodie asked Doyle as the taxi crossed over Vauxhall Bridge and began to wind northward through the city toward Hyde Park and the Parkway Hotel.

"I said Jamieson was a rich relative from the States over here on business. I told him I'd just had a transatlantic call from his wife who was trying to locate him because his Manhattan doctor accidentally prescribed the wrong heart tablets and it could be dangerous if he took them for too long. I don't know who Cowley gave the job to but the information was certainly quick enough coming back."

"He couldn't have been quicker if the queen had been kidnapped," said Bodie with a grin.

The taxi drew up outside the Parkway and the two men hurried up the broad marble steps and across the lobby to the reception desk. "What can I do for you?" asked the receptionist.

"We're looking for Mister Jamieson," said Doyle.

"And who shall I say is here?"

"Tell him it's Charles and Maxwell Kinross and that it's urgent. Tell him we have more news on this morning's deal. He'll know what you mean."

The receptionist pressed a number of buttons on a console and spoke quietly into a mouthpiece on the desk. After listening a moment she said to Bodie and Doyle, "Mister Jamieson would like you to go up. He's in room two hundred and seven on the seventeenth floor."

Bodie thanked her and they stepped into the lift. He pressed a button and the lift doors closed. They ascended in silence, each man preparing himself mentally, feeling a looseness in his limbs, flexing then relaxing his muscles, feeling the weight of his gun, first in the right hand, then the left.

At the seventeenth floor the lift doors opened on an empty corridor. The two men, tense and prepared, hurried quickly to the door of room 207. Bodie nodded and then half crouched, his gun held at shoulder height. Doyle moved out of line of fire from the door, pressed his back to the wall, leaned to his right to knock softly on the door, then waited.

It was easier than they had expected. Jamieson opened the door fractionally and peered suspiciously through the crack. But before he could level his gun at either of the C.I.5. men Bodie had kicked the door back into his face. Jamieson stumbled backward, the gun exploding as he fell, the bullet smashing into the glass chandelier above his head. Before he could fire again Doyle kicked the gun from his hand while Bodie stood astride him.

From behind a locked door came the sound of banging and muffled cries. Doyle went to open it and saw a curly blonde in red tank top and blue jeans. Though she was bound and gagged she was still kicking furiously at the back of the door. "You must be Miss Moorhouse," Doyle said smiling gently as he knelt to untie her.

* * * * * * * * *

"What are you doing back so soon?" asked Cowley in surprise as Bodie and Doyle entered his office with Jamieson and Miss Moorhouse.

"Chief, I'd like you to meet Wilbur Jamieson," said Doyle.

"Ah, your Uncle. Glad to see they found you in time, Mister Jamieson. What can I do for you?"

"He's not my uncle and you can lock him up," said Doyle.

Cowley's expression changed rapidly from astonished to amused, then to incredulous, and then angry. "What in the name of heaven do you want me to charge him with, Doyle?"

"Trying to tip the nuclear balance. If you can't find anything on the statutes that covers that then try kidnapping."

"My father is Professor Carl Moorhouse, he designed the warheads on the latest American missiles," explained Miss Moorhouse. "Jamieson used to work on the project but he was unreliable and incompetent. Eventually he was fired. He always blamed daddy for it and so he devised a plan to kidnap me while I was here in London on my summer vacation. He thought that by threatening my life he could force my father to hand over the designs of the warheads."

"And then he'd make a pretty penny selling them to the highest bidders," said Cowley, rubbing his chin thoughtfully. "But how did you two get on to him?"

"You sure you want to hear?"

Cowley nodded.

"First of all there are a few more things you should know. There's a gambling club South of the river called the Blue Cockatoo. You'll find the owners locked in a broom cupboard there. They were in on the kidnapping. And there's an insurance clerk called Pebblewhite who likes to lose his money on the Cockatoo's tables. You could pick him up too."

"That's if Angela Babcock hasn't already killed him," smiled Doyle.

Cowley looked confused.

"Who's Angela Babcock?" he asked.

"A holidaymaker from Leeds. She was down here on a mini weekend."

Cowley put his head into his hands. "On second thoughts don't tell me," he muttered.

"On one condition, chief," said Bodie cheerfully.

"What's that?"

"That you don't send us on another holiday."

"Yeah," said Doyle, "they're almost as hectic as working."

FAKING A FIGHT

One of the ingredients which adds extra excitement to The Professionals programme each week is action-packed scuffle — usually with Bodie and Doyle handing it out and a villain or two coming off worst.

It all looks so real as the fists fly and no doubt lots of young fans play-act the battles in the school playground afterwards.

It's no secret that punches are pulled on films but it takes a special sort of expertise to put together an action-packed fight and make it look good under the probing eye of the TV camera.

Behind the fight sequence, and incidentally all the other dangerous looking stunts in the series, is a man whose job is as exciting and dangerous as it sounds. He is Peter Brayham, the Action Arranger.

This is his story about how he puts the Wham! Bang! Wallop! into the programmes.

"First thing I do," says Peter, "is to read the script and find out about the story and the characters involved.

"I have to put together a fight sequence that will suit the story and fit in with the background of the characters in it. I have to look at his lifestyle and think what sort of fighting ability he would have. Is he an SAS man? If he is, he would use unarmed combat techniques. Is he a street fighter? Is he a villain?

"Doyle is a karate expert so I can include karate moves for him. Bodie is ex-SAS. In fact, both Martin and Lewis are so good at fight sequences now that I talk to them as though they were stuntmen.

"With new actors to the series, I have to get their confidence before we can work together. I have already developed the fight on paper and in my mind before we start so next I play the part of the baddie myself to show them how it's done.

"It's easy for them to copy people because they are trained to act, but now I have to show them how to act the part not with words but physically.

"I wouldn't encourage anyone to copy anything we do because accidents can so easily happen.

"And no one must ever try falling through windows or out of moving vehicles. Again, the dangerous stunts like those look easy but they aren't."

Here's a little secret you might watch out for next time you watch the programme — in the credits at the beginning of the programme, it's Peter who crashes through the plate glass window.

And that was a 25ft by 25ft window of two inches thick plate glass! "It only took 20 minutes to actually do the shot," he says, "but believe me, it's a dangerous trick for anyone.

"But a stuntman is not a man who takes risks, he's the one who eliminates them."

"Each fight is a choreographed sequence of moves, in the same way as a dance routine. We practise it very slowly at first and if I see that an actor has a particular weakness — say he's not too good with his left or with his legs — then I take out any moves involving them.

"It's far better to watch 15 moves — or numbers as we call them — expertly done than to watch 50 which are not."

"I know that when you see a fight on the screen, it may look very simple and easy but believe me a lot of work has to go into it first.

"There is a genuine aspect of danger too for in The Professionals, we often use real weapons for authenticity, and if an actor hasn't been briefed properly, his career could be over for good.

"I would never want anything like that on my conscience so I am fanatical about safety. I have been rehearsing stunts for 25 years and I give the actors the benefit of all the experience I have acquired but sometimes, even so, we can get the odd occasion where someone actually does hit someone else and hurt them.

"It doesn't happen on a 'take' but in the rehearsals when we are still putting it all together.

WORD SEARCH

Here's a MINDBENDER for you! It's a crossword with a difference — we give all the answers! What you have to do is fit the right words into the right squares so that it all makes sense!

GUN
SPY

CODE
FILM
HERO

MARK ONE
MYSTERY.
TALL MEN
VIEWERS

ACTION
ACTORS
BLANKS
DANGER
EXTRAS
HIJACK
MAGNUM
STUDIO
TIMING

BANGS
CHIEF
CRIME
DRAMA
PROPS
RADIO
RIFLE
SIEGE
SMOKE
STORY

CAR CRASH
DIRECTOR
FILM CREW
INTRIGUE
PRODUCER
SOUNDMEN
STUNTMEN
TEAM WORK

ADVENTURE
CAMERAMAN
TOUGH GUYS
TOP SECRET

EXPLOSIVES
HELICOPTER
MASTERMIND

MAKE UP ARTIST
SPECIAL AGENT
TRANSMITTORS

SECRET SERVICE

SPECIAL EFFECTS

CONTINUITY GIRLS

THE PROFESSIONALS

CRIMINAL INTELLIGENCE

WORD SEARCH

Here's a giant Word Search Puzzle. Let's see how good you are at following the clues and finding the words. As you find each word, draw a loop around it with a pencil or pen.

```
L S E R U T N E U D A E I D O B M A I L L I W S W
C O S K N A L B A A D S T C E F F E L A I C E P S
M R N F E I H C T N E G A L A I C E P S A M A T P
E Y E D B B T L Y K C A J I H L X L R C C A P I Y
C X S W O O T A P P A S S Y T M S T O M T G O N Y
I G T T R N A P K I H I S H O T T E T A R N N U E
V E V R E N W P E E E E S G P O U N E R E U S M S
R R K C A R T E G G O M R N S U N S C T S M I G I
E C R O F S Y R E G O N W I E G T I T I S R N O N
S Y R E V A R B B K I K E N C H M O I N C A S D O
T R D N U O S O E O E O B I R G E N O S B O T N R
E O K O O R C A N L L N A A E U N P N H S P A I H
R T P E L F I R A D I O D R T Y S Q U A D R R M C
C S S P E D L D E T O N A T E S S R E W E I V R N
E N E C S I S H S H H C E G E O R G E C O W L E Y
S E X A T R T T C A C L P A E L O E U N M I S T S
R I P M N E U R R U N I I N I L E D A A N U N S S
O R L E E C D A I E U M S O S O O V R T S O E A N
T E O R M T I I P P P A O I P R S K I P T O M M I
T T S A U O O L T R A X D T P R O G E S Y C E T L
I P I M C R X E T O H S E A A N U N E T I D L X L
M O V E O B O R P P F F C C E E S C E T O O C X O
S C E N D L M I S S I O N O E E U F T C A T N O C
N I S D O O D T E L L U B L R R A N O I T C A D S
A L E R T W R R T N E M N G I S S A G N I M I T I
R E E C R Y M R A E V I F T F E L Y O D Y A R N W
T H E R E G N A D M O N Y R O T A R O B A L B U E
E N O H P O R C I M A N O S K C A J N O D R O G L
```

CLUES

ACTION
ACTOR
ACTRESS
ADVENTURES
ALERT
ARMY
ASSIGNMENT
BANGS
BLANKS
BLOW
BRAVERY
BRIAN CLEMENS
BULLET
CAMERAMAN
CARS
CHIEF
CLAPPERBOARD
CLIMAX
CODE
CONTACT
CREW
CRIME
CROOK
CYPHER
DANGER
DETONATE
DIRECTOR
DOCUMENTS
DRAMA
EPISODE
EXPERTS
EXPLOSIVES
EXTRAS
FILE
FILM
FIRE
FIVE
FORCE
GEORGE COWLEY
GORDON JACKSON
GUN
HELICOPTER
HERO
HIJACK
LABORATORY
LEAP
LEWIS COLLINS
LOCATION
LONDON WEEKEND TELEVISION
MAGNUM
MARK ONE
MARTIN SHAW
MASTERMIND
MICROPHONE
MISSION
MYSTERY
PASS
PRODUCER
PROPS
PROTECTION
PUNCH
RADIO
RAY DOYLE
RIFLE
SAFETY
SCENE
SCRIPT
SECRET SERVICE
SECURITY
SHOT
SIEGE
SMOKE
SOUND
SPECIAL AGENT
SPECIAL EFFECTS
SPY
SQUAD
STAR
STORY
STUDIO
STUNTMEN
SUSPENSE
SYNCHRONISE
TAKE ONE
TENSION
TIMING
TOP SECRET
TOUGH GUYS
TRACK
TRAILER
TRAINING
TRANSMITTOR
UNIT
VIEWERS
WEAPONS
WEB
WILLIAM BODIE

AGENT DOYLE

AGENT BODIE

LUCKY BREAK

Professionals fan, Pat Smith, of Forres, Moray, Scotland, won a super electric portable typewriter, in a short-story writing competition in "The Professionals" magazine. Pat, who is a 33-year old housewife, has written another exciting CI5 story especially for The Professionals Annual.

George Cowley looked up as Bodie and Doyle entered his office. He decided to get straight to the point: "The Gower boys have friends they didn't tell us about — Alan Blair and Gerry Frost." He paused, then continued gravely: "A short while ago, they abducted the minister's niece. They want the Gowers released by mid-day tomorrow or they'll kill her."

Cowley looked at Bodie.

But it was Doyle who asked: "How old is she?"

"Twenty-three."

"So, where do we start?" asked Bodie.

Questioning the Gower brothers got them nowhere.

Hours ticked by. They had no leads on Blair and Frost.

Bodie and Doyle snatched a few hours' sleep before an early-morning meeting in Cowley's office.

"Four hours before they call to arrange the exchange and we still don't know who they are," said Cowley anxiously.

Bodie shrugged. "Well, they've got no form."

"Unless that's not their real names," suggested Doyle.

"Shall we persuade the Gowers to talk?" asked Bodie, rubbing his fist meaningfully.

Cowley considered for a while; made up his mind, and issued a string of orders.

The rendezvous was arranged for eleven-thirty.

At ten-thirty, two Cortinas followed by Bodie's silver-grey Capri approached the isolated spot. Cowley intended to stake out the area — but his plan had been anticipated.

Frost focused his binoculars as the cars came into view. He jumped down from his vantage-point and ran back to the waiting car, yelling to Blair.

The first Cortina turned into the clearing — just as a red car streaked out and hared off.

Doyle saw. And Bodie squeezed their car past the second Cortina and gave chase.

The lane, strewn with autumn leaves, was narrow and twisty. Doyle glimpsed the red car up ahead. It turned left.

Bodie was driving fast. Too fast —

The turning was concealed. Bodie braked, spinning the wheel. The Capri did a neat one-eighty degree turn — and stalled.

Bodie cursed, and glanced at Doyle whose face registered a look of disgust to match his own.

They wasted only seconds, but it was enough. The red car was gone. There were no more turnings and Bodie belted the car along, hoping to catch up.

Without warning, the windscreen shattered with a tremendous bang. Bodie hit the brakes. Another explosive bang followed. The car shuddered and slewed wildly. Bodie wrestled with the steering, fighting to keep the car straight.

He lost the fight.

The car slammed sideways into the left-hand bank. Doyle's head clashed painfully with the side window. And before Bodie could recover from the impact, the door was flung open and a hand grabbed his shoulder.

He tensed, preparing to free himself.

Something glinted in the sunlight.

Bodie relaxed. He was in no position to make a fight of it. His movements would be restricted. And a knife could do a lot of damage in that situation.

Frost hauled Bodie from the car.

Now, Bodie calculated. He started to move — and crumpled to the ground, struck from behind by Blair.

Doyle was still slumped in his seat. Blair decided to leave him and helped Frost drag Bodie to their car. They bundled him in and drove off at speed.

Ray Doyle came to. He rubbed his head — and wished he hadn't.

"Bodie?"

Doyle struggled out of the car and looked around.

No sign of Bodie.

The damaged Capri had come to rest almost opposite a lay-by. Muddy tyre-tracks led away up the road.

Realization dawned. Doyle reached for the radio.

"4.5 to Alpha."

"Doyle, what's —"

Doyle cut in: "We were ambushed. They've taken Bodie."

"What!" Cowley's voice erupted. "Where are you?"

Cowley checked the map, then told Doyle: "There are three farms nearby. Check them out. I'll join you."

Ignoring his thumping headache Doyle changed the damaged wheel, and knocked out the windscreen. As he drove towards the nearest farmhouse, he wondered if Bodie was alright.

Blair contacted Cowley again.

"Very stupid, Mr. Cowley," he said mockingly. "Now we have two hostages."

"If y. . ."

"We'll give you another chance. But no more tricks. Listen carefully . . ."

Cowley listened. He didn't like the way things were going. He needed time. Then, Blair unwittingly gave him a vital clue which confirmed his hunch.

There was nothing suspicious about Southdene Farm and Doyle enquired about the other two farms. Mrs. Howard told him there was no-one at Eastgate at present. She pointed across the fields . . .

"That's strange. That red car was there yesterday —"

"Thanks," yelled Doyle, running back to his car.

Bodie became aware of his surroundings and struggled to sit up. With Susan's help, he freed himself from his bonds. Quickly, as he untied Susan, he explained exactly what he wanted her to do.

Blair looked at Frost. "Sounds like he's awake. Go up and check him."

Frost was unprepared for what he saw — the open window and knotted sheet. The moment of hesitation was enough for Bodie. He pounded, from behind the door, striking Frost as he turned. Falling with him. Rolling. Then, Bodie was on his feet and hauling Frost up.

Blair appeared in the doorway, Bodie's Browning auto in his fist. Bodie thrust Frost at him. They sprawled onto the landing. Frost tumbled down the stairs.

Cowley met Doyle at the end of the track leading to Eastgate Farm. The hedgerow afforded them cover as they crept up to the house.

Doyle kicked in the front door as Frost was starting upstairs with the rifle. He dropped it and surrendered quietly. Doyle left him to Cowley, and ran upstairs.

Bodie was trading punches with Blair.

A vicious blow left Bodie momentarily breathless and Blair dived for the fallen gun.

It slithered away.

He looked up and saw Doyle's gun snouting down at him...

"Thanks," Bodie gasped.

He drew a deep steadying breath. Then he walked across to the built-in cupboard and helped Susan out.

Cowley was justifiably pleased and, favouring Bodie and Doyle with a warm smile, he said: "Well done lads."

BEHIND THE SCENES

Working in the world of filming is a fascinating and satisfying job for everyone on a film unit from the actors on one side of the camera to the host of technical experts on the other side.

We thought you might like to go behind the scenes and find out a little about a few of the exciting jobs in filming.

Here we talk to some of the experts from Mark One Productions, who have been working on "The Professionals" series.

SOUND

When it comes to the recording of the sound for "The Professionals", special talents and equipment are needed for the methods used are different to those of most films.

The sound is recorded 'live' and not post-synchronised - added on afterwards in a special studio. Head of the Sound Crew is David Crozier, who operates the sophisticated equipment stacked on the special mobile trolley pictured here.

The trolley itself is an invention which grew out of "The Professionals" series and the problems the Sound Men faced. The main problem David found was that the filming moves from one location to another frequently — sometimes four times in one day.

He needed equipment, therefore, which could be packed up quickly and moved on and which could be ready to go again in record time.

Bit by bit, more refinements have been added to the trolley and now it even has a large striped fishing umbrella for work on rainy days!

If you're a bit of a sound buff, here's some info which might interest you. The machine which records the sound is a NAGRA tape recorder using ¼ inch tape and by means of a mixer panel, it can take up to seven different microphones at one time.

What it records is later linked to the film which has been shot by a special crystal pulse recorded on a special sound track running down the centre of the tape.

This track is then used by the transfer machine back at the laboratories to transfer accurately the sound onto a 16mm separate magnetic track used in editing.

"It's very much like a domestic tape recorder," says David, "but upgraded. It's highly sophisticated. For instance, it will work at any temperature in any condition and still be reliable. It will even run in the rain safely and it can be used in conditions of high vibration like in the back of a car going at speed or an aeroplane going into a dive or rolling."

Another problem of recording live is that the sensitive microphones will pick up any sound, whether it is part of the filming or not! An aeroplane suddenly passing overhead will stop the filming. Even a dog barking or birds singing could mean the whole crew coming to a standstill until the unrehearsed 'noise' ceases.

The Sound Crew are also responsible for hiding away tiny microphones on the actors so that they can't be seen by the viewers. Even that requires lots of skill for if they are placed against prickly or abrasive clothing, the rubbing sound as it chafes against the microphone will be picked up on the tape too!

While Bodie and Doyle and the brave men of CI5 constantly hold the safety of nations in their hands, there's one man who is often responsible for the lives of the whole of "The Professionals".

His nickname is Dr Death but though his job is a dangerous one, that name was only given to him as a joke — honestly!

He is Mike Collins, who is in charge of creating special effects for the programmes, like the mind-blowing explosions as a bomb rips a car into thousands of pieces or bullet holes riddling into woodwork and blood splattering as they hit home.

Mike is the envy of thousands of young schoolboys who dream of doing a job like his. But in reality, the glamour of the job is perhaps as big an illusion as the illusions Mike himself creates for the screen!

"There's more hard work than glamour" says Mike. "But special effects men do suffer from first night nerves just like actors." Mike has worked on many films as well as on "The Professionals" series — he's been in the business for 30 years.

"I was physically sick when we blew up the

SPECIAL EFFECTS

chateau in the film 'Dirty Dozen'" he says, "but the elation after it's all over is so great that you suffer nearly as much as you do before it happens!

"You check and check and check again to make sure nothing can go wrong. You start to shake because you are concentrating so much. You are continuously checking the fireboard which is the triggerpoint. Then it's the countdown. You hit the button and it's gone."

That's creating a big explosion. What about blowing up cars? Is that an illusion too? "We really do blow them up and we need to know exactly where the camera crew can safely be placed without being hit by debris.

"We use what's called 'a ringer' car. We find a car which is identical to the one being driven in the episode. Usually, it's a new car which has been written off. We find them in breakers' yards and in fact we have a man whose job is being in charge of matching up ringer vehicles."

What about letting us into one or two secrets?

"Well, take a bullet hole in a door," he said. "This effect is created by a highly sophisticated detonator which is specially designed for motion pictures and special effects work. In reality, when a bullet hits a door, it enters from the side of the door facing the gun and takes the debris from the woodwork with it.

"What you actually seen on the screen, however, is the debris being blown out forwards but it happens so quickly that it looks real. The detonator is actually behind the door."

What does it take to make a good special effects man? "Intelligence, inventiveness and being a good model maker" says Mike. "You need to have a flair for special effects."

MAKE UP

Being a make-up girl for the stars is many a young girl's dream and imagine what it would be like if the stars were Gordon Jackson, Martin Shaw and Lewis Collins!

Sue Black doesn't have to imagine — she knows for she is one of the make-up girls who has worked on "The Professionals" series.

So how do you get a job like that? And is it really a glamorous life? What are the stars really like? These are the questions Sue gets asked all the time and, of course, they are the questions we want the answers to too.

Sue works as a freelance make-up artist which means she is self employed and is hired by film companies for specific series or films.

She used to work as a beautician in a famous London store then she saw a newspaper advertisement for trainees for the BBC make-up department. She was lucky enough to be chosen and after a period of working in television on programmes like "Pebble Mill" and "The Benny Hill Show", she decided to branch out on her own.

Luck was on Sue's side again and after only one telephone call to a film company, she was working.

Ask her about the glamour and she will soon put you right. She has to get up as early as 5.30am and drive off to the first location Mark One Productions are working on that day.

By 8am, she and hairdresser, Sue Love, will be hard at work getting the first actors called ready for filming. They work in a caravan, half of which is a dressing room.

Sue says, "you have got to be a different sort of person to someone who clings to a staff job. You end up in amazing places. It's not knowing where you are going to be and what you are going to be

BEHIND THE SCENES ....

CAMERAS

called upon to do that is the exciting thing about this job."

Sue once had to put rubber waders on and wade out into the sea to attend to Hattie Jaques' make-up as she was being filmed on a raft!

But back to our men from CI5! Do they have any 'beauty secrets' which need disguising with lots of stage make-up? "Not at all" says Sue. "I use the minimum of make-up on everyone. I use Max Factor Pan-stick a lot because it is light in texture."

In fact, Lewis and Martin both have good clear skins. Their only problem is that they do have heavy beard lines, especially at the end of the day, but Sue always has electric razors on hand.

"Gordon is no problem either. He likes to look natural and healthy."

When Sue is not doing make-ups in the caravan, she is never far away from the cameras, waiting to be called, for apart from what you might call a 'straight' make-up, she also has to create cuts, bruises, scratches, black eyes after fights, explosions, car crashes and the like. And then when the filming switches to another scene, she often has to remove the 'injuries' and clean up the actors again!

There is, of course, long periods when she simply has to sit around and wait. That could prove very boring and uncomfortable in excessively hot or cold weather, but it's all part of the life that Sue loves.

Although only one man actually operates a film camera in action, it takes a whole team of people to carry out the work of the camera section of the Mark One Productions film unit.

"The Professionals" episodes are shot on 16mm films whereas feature films are put onto 35mm or 70mm film. Apart from the economical advantages, 16mm lens gives a greater depth of field and the cameras are lighter to handle — an important factor when you need to get a camera inside the back of a car, or in a bedroom cupboard, or when location is changing three times daily. The 16mm film is providing better quality viewing than the American rivals are achieving with their 35mm format. Word has it that they are constantly amazed at the quality of the British work, despite the amount of short, dark days that our climate provides on location!

John Maskell, one of the camera operators who has worked on "The Professionals" series, says "The operator has to work very closely with the director but he relies heavily on good teamwork from the camera crew.

"You sometimes have to coax the actors into the best position for the camera but most of the time, you have to use your skill to adjust to them. Whatever happens you have to make sure that you don't inhibit them.

"The trouble with me" he laughs, "is that when I get my eye to a camera, I think I'm invisible. If there happens to be a stray missile about, I tend to ignore it and think it can't possibly hurt me because I'm behind the cameras. Luckily, there's usually someone around to snatch me out of harm's way if I get too involved in filming to notice what's really happening."

Chris Sargent is what's called a Focus Puller. "I am responsible for the equipment" he says. "I have to make sure that everything is there that is supposed to be there and that it is all cleaned and ready to use.

"Then during the rehearsal, I have to work out what the focus needs to be depending on what's going to be happening on the eventual shot.

"I get told what the exposure is and I have to make sure the right filter is on. And make sure there isn't a hair in the gate — in other words that there are no 'foreign bodies' which will eventually appear on your screen when they are not supposed to be there."

Dusty Miller is the Lighting Cameraman. He creates the mood for the scene to be shot. He has to know the limitations of the lighting equipment used and has to balance that against the daylight available. Sometimes, he has to use his skills to 'create' daylight situations when the light of the day is fading.

He often has to use visual aids like coloured gels or smoke, perhaps to create a late night club scene where the room is full of cigarette smoke.

Peter Hall is what's called a Grip. His special responsibilities are for the bits and pieces like handles, dollies (which the camera 'sits' on) and rails which are used for the camera to 'track' along whilst it's in action.

And then there's the Clapperboard. You've seen the chap who clicks a board and says "Take One!". That's Joe Hidderley's job and it's a vital one too.

It's the snapping noise made by that board which enables the laboratory technicians to synchronise the film and the sound.

He also has to phone the laboratories each day to get a report on the film which has been rushed in the day before. He has to keep the magazines loaded with one roll of film at a time and keep a written record of everything that is shot.

And he even makes sure the cameramen are kept supplied with tea and rolls!

It's quite fascinating just how much work goes in behind the cameras. If you're a keen photographer, you might like to know that most of the cameras used are ARRIFLEX 16SR cameras, made by a major German manufacturer of professional 16mm equipment.

This crew use two types of cameras, one of which is 'blimped' (padded) to cut down as much noise as possible while it is running, and up to four cameras at a time are used on the action sequences.

The crew shoot, on average, eight rolls of film a day, which means in the usual ten day period it takes to shoot one episode of "The Professionals" they have gone through 30,000 feet of film.

Much of this ends up on the cutting room floor, however, as only a total of five and a half rolls are needed to make a 55 minute episode. It takes 400 feet of film for ten minutes' viewing.

The unit aim to complete five minutes of screen time each day, which to you may seem so little but in fact most feature films only complete 90 seconds of screen time out of each full day's shooting. Mark One have even topped nine minutes a day on occasions! Just goes to show what experts they are!

THE ONE THAT GOT AWAY

Transport arrives . . .
JUMP!
Escape!
Later, in George Cowley's office . . .
THE RAY BROTHERS! THEY'RE VERY NAUGHTY BOYS INDEED.
MASTERS HAS ESCAPED... ALONG WITH THE RAY BROTHERS
EXACTLY, THERE'LL BE A STRONG POLICE PRESENCE. YOU'LL HAVE TO CO-OPERATE.
DO YOU THINK THE FOUR OF THEM WILL STICK TOGETHER?
MESSAGE FOR YOU MR COWLEY.
I DON'T KNOW, YOU'RE GOING TO HAVE TO PLAY THIS ONE BY EAR.
THEY'VE FOUND THE GETAWAY VAN. GET OVER THERE RIGHT AWAY.
Inside the van, police make a grisly discovery . . .
IT'S THE DRIVER HIS THROAT'S BEEN CUT!
SEEMS LIKE THE RAY BROTHERS HAVEN'T CHANGED A BIT.

YOU'RE NOT NEEDED HERE THIS IS POLICE BUSINESS
MASTERS IS OUR BUSINESS, AND IF WE FIND THE RAY BROTHERS–WE'LL FIND HIM.
WELL I DON'T WANT ANY COWBOYS ON THIS CASE SERGEANT WILLIS HERE WILL ACCOMPANY YOU
IF YOU SAY SO – COME ON SARGE!
Later...
WE'VE DONE A COMPLETE RUN DOWN ON THE RAYS. IT SEEMS JOE'S BROTHER IN LAW HAS A SMALL FLAT... 133 LANCASTRIA BUILDINGS
WE'LL CHECK IT OUT
Lancastria buildings...
WHAT DO YOU THINK?
THE RAYS WILL NEED NEW CLOTHES. WE'LL TAKE THE STAIRS SARGE, YOU WATCH THE REAR DOORS
OK
IT SHOULD BE ON THE NEXT FLOOR
Suddenly...
GET BACK COPPERS
WE SAID GET BACK
THIS WAY BOYS —LENNIE COM-ON
I'LL COVER FOR YOU

BETTER TURN IT IN LENNIE
YOUR'E NOT TAKING ME BACK
I'M NEVER GOING BACK
OOF!
AAAARCH
YOU OK ?
YEAH BUT I WONDER HOW THE SARGE IS GETTING ON WITH THE OTHER
The question is soon answered . . .
COUNT YOURSELF LUCKY YOU DIDN'T GET SHOT
THAT SPY FELLA HIT ME OVER THE HEAD
SKREEE!
STREWTH! THEY'VE GOT THEMSELVES A MERC! COME ON
WE'LL NEVER CATCH THEM IN THIS
WE'LL TRY!

Doyle's brilliant driving manages to close the gap . . .
ONCE THEY HIT THE MOTORWAY— WE'VE LOST THEM
HOLD ONTO YOUR HAT
WHA...T?
CRUNCH!
COME ON LETS GET OUT OF HERE
JOE, SLOW DOWN MY LEG — I THINK IT'S BROKEN
WE CAN'T SHOOT WITH THOSE KIDS ABOUT.
AND WE'VE GOT TO FIND ANOTHER MOTOR
JOE PLEASE I CAN'T
GET IN OR LET GO OF THAT DOOR
SO LONG LOSER
JOE PLEASE ...I... UGH!

HEY WHATS ALL THIS ABOUT ?
WE'LL EXPLAIN LATER !
The chase is joined once more...
CRASH
THEY'VE GOT A CHOPPER - STEP ON IT
GET THIS THING OUT OF HERE
But...
And...
OOF!

As the chopper takes off . . .
DOYLE YOU'VE DONE ENOUGH MATE, LET GO BEFORE IT'S TOO LATE.
HANG ON YOU FLAMING IDIOT
And . . .
OOCH
SPLOSH!
LOOKS LIKE YOUR PALS ALRIGHT
HE ALWAYS WAS A SHOWER
But Joe Ray is not so lucky . . .
OUT!
BUT-BUT
AAAAUGH!
OUT
YEAH WE WON'T CATCH HIM NOW
I CAN'T SAY I'M SORRY ABOUT THE RAY BROTHERS BUT IT LOOKS LIKE MASTERS GOT AWAY

And, in Cowley's office . . .
SO THE OPERATION WAS SUCCESSFUL AFTER ALL.
YEAH, NO ONE WILL SUSPECT MASTERS IS WITH US AFTER ALL THAT
AND HE'LL BE FREE TO FEED US ALL THOSE LOVELY SECRETS
IF THE RAY BROTHERS HADN'T BUTTED IN, THAT DRIVER WOULD STILL BE ALIVE.
IT'S A PITY JOE RAY WAS AN ANIMAL.
MASTERS PAID HIM OFF THOUGH — IN FULL
YES, THE DRIVER KNEW THE RISKS. I WANT YOU TWO BACK HERE AT NINE TOMORROW WITH A FULL WRITTEN REPORT.
And . . .
YOU WERE GRANDSTANDING A BIT WEREN'T YOU? WHY DIDN'T YOU LET GO OF THE CHOPPER EARLIER?
WELL I HATE TO ADMIT IT MATE BUT I COULDN'T — MY JACKET GOT STUCK.

The Park

Sitting waiting in the park,
It's freezing cold and getting dark,
"I'm cold," says Bodie with dismay
Looking to his good friend, Ray.
"I know how you feel, Bodie, mate.
"It's half-past-eight and Cowley's late."
"Oh, come on, Ray, this is stupid
Sitting here playing Cupid."
"Ay! You're right. I feel the same.
"It's Cowley's fault. He's to blame!"
Off they go at a run
But they're too late, there's a man with a gun
Waiting for them at the gate,
Shouting words of abuse and hate.
"What's all this then?" Ray says calmly.
"Don't ask me, mate. This man's barmy."
Rooted now to the ground,
Not a word, not a sound.
Bodie whispers "We could rush him but he looks frisky"
"Phew!" says Doyle, "That could be risky."
Bodie smiles with a grin
"I think I know how we can win."
Before Ray has time to look around
"Cops!" shouts Bodie. "Hit the ground!"
The man, bewildered, turns his back
And Bodie grabs him like a sack.
The man drops down but he's not through,
For jumping like a kangaroo
He wallops Bodie — on the nose.
Bodie's now lying on the ground,
Confusion and noise all around.
Doyle, who thinks this is not his idea of fun,
Runs to the gate to pick up the gun.
It's very dark with a slight breeze.
Doyle looks to the man and he shouts "Freeze!"
The man turns round, it's the end of his game.
Doyle with the gun asks him his name.
Before he can answer, there's the sound of a car.
Bodie and Doyle know it's not very far.
Out of the dark comes Cowley so cool
In a car from the CI5 Motoring Pool.
His leg's playing up, he's not very pleased,
He's got a bad cold
And he's wanting to sneeze.
Bodie now cries "It's all clear!
That man was Tommy Deer!"
"Tommy Deer" says Colwey abrupt
"Yes. The copper we put away for being corrupt."
Off they go into the night
Bodie in pain from the fight.
It's all over. The story is told.
The lights have gone out. It's very cold.

"The Park" was written by 20-year old Alison Burman, of Penarth, Glamorgan, South Wales. It was the winning entry in a CI5 poetry competition in "The Professionals" magazine and Alison's prize was a sweat shirt which was actually worn by her hero, Martin Shaw, in a Professionals episode.

ACTION with BODIE & DOYLE

THE EMBASSY INCIDENT

Cowley's car turned into Pickwick Street and slowed to a halt a discreet distance from the Embassy. He gestured vaguely with his right hand as his left opened the suitcase on the seat beside him and began searching for some documents.

"Take a good look," said Cowley over his shoulder, "I'll give you plans of the inside later."

Bodie and Doyle studied the tall building with the large green and red flag over the door. On the first floor balcony a huge poster of a man in a uniform covered with medals drooped in the afternoon rain. A banner hung from the balustrade proclaiming FAISAK: SAVIOUR OF THE PEOPLE in both English and Arabic.

"Seems a popular sort of fellow," observed Bodie.

"He has a simple method of staying that way."

"What's that?"

"He has anyone who disagrees with him killed."

"It's one way to run a country, I suppose," said Doyle.

"It's why so many of his people have fled the country. But even then, his critics aren't safe. Faisak's secret police are sent after them." Cowley brought a folder from his suitcase. "It seems our General is a sensitive wee chappie — critics seem to bring the worst out of him, even from long distances. Listen to this . . ." Cowley began reading aloud from the folder.

"New York, September: Two outspoken exiles shot dead on a Bronx subway. Paris, November: Attempted poisoning of an exiled family. London, November: Former leader's son falls from penthouse window. Rome, December: Exiled couple disappear. Cowley put the folder down . . . "There's plenty more."

"They're either bumped off or taken

back home to stand trial for treason. When they're found guilty, they get shot. Quite a card is Faisak," said Doyle.

"But why should this concern CI5?" asked Bodie.

Cowley opened another folder and handed them a photograph.

"This is Professor Haroun Rashid," he said. "A scientist. He fled to England five years ago after Faisak's men killed his wife and children. He was granted asylum and given protection. He began working for the Nuclear Fuels Advisory Commission, and did very well for himself. Had access to some extremely sensitive information."

"Like where to find the makings of a nuclear bomb?"

"Among other things. Faisak is openly hostile to our country. If he could find out the weak spots in our nuclear power stations he could cause us a lot of aggravation."

"But Rashid wouldn't tell him anything, would he?" asked Doyle.

"Not voluntarily. The trouble is . . . Haroud Rashid disappeared three days ago."

"You reckon they've snatched him?"

"Looks like it. He told a colleague that two of Faisak's men had been following him the day before he disappeared."

"We're too late then," said Bodie, "they'll have him back home by now."

"Or dead," said Doyle.

"We don't think so," said Cowley. "We think they've got him stashed away in the Embassy there."

"Then it's stalemate," said Bodie. "They can't get him out of the country with us watching and we can't get inside because of international law."

Bodie studied Cowley's humourless smile and realised the danger of the forthcoming assignment.

"The Embassy may be out of bounds to CI5," said Cowley, "but since when did two fanatical terrorists pay attention to international law?"

Cowley started up the car and began the drive back to his office. On the way, he explained his plans.

"You get inside the building," said the Scot, "take the entire staff hostage then issue your demands. When these are refused you negotiate. Then you release some prisoners in exchange for concessions."

"What are our demands?"

"It doesn't matter. Just make sure you release Rashid. As soon as you've done that, you can surrender."

"Too simple," said Bodie.

"It can work," argued Cowley as

they pulled up in the car park. He led them to the sliding doors of the basement weapons room. "Keep the hostages away from the window and I'll get the press to leave it alone. No-one will be any the wiser."

Inside the weapons room, the noise was deafening. On the practice ranges other CI5 agents fired at moving shadow targets and Cowley had to shout to make himself heard over the staccato explosions of their weapons. They approached a bench where a technician was working on a row of grenades. Cowley indicated a large green shoulder bag.

"Twenty-eight sticks of dynamite, fuses, detonators and eight grenades," he explained.

"What's he doing with the grenades?" asked Doyle, nodding toward the technician.

"He's making them safe. Taking the detonators out. The dynamite's already safe — it's made out of plasticine."

"Safe for whom?" asked Bodie.

"Safe for everyone. The people in the Embassy will never know the explosives aren't real."

"Maybe we should tell them," said Doyle with a grim smile. "After all, we don't want an unfair advantage."

That night Bodie and Doyle set out. Their first inkling that something was wrong came when they found no guard on the Embassy door. He was inside the darkened hallway with a big red hole where his left eye should have been. Bodie bent over the body, and was about to speak when a blinding flash of pain exploded at the base of his skull and fireworks started going off all over his brain.

When he came to, Bodie was still in the hallway. The lights were on and he was staring down the barrel of a Kalashnikov. A hooded figure held the rifle in shaking hands. Against the opposite wall, Doyle stood with his hands held high above his head.

"You're not going to believe this, mate," said Doyle, ignoring the second hooded figure, who was prodding him in the ribs with another Kalashnikov, "but these jokers have beaten us to the punch. The Cow's got a real siege on his hands."

The second man gave Doyle another prod. His voice was on the verge of hysteria.

"Do not speak! Do not move! You are the prisoners of the People's Liberation Army. Understand that we wish you no harm personally, but if you no obey — we kill you!"

Bodie groaned as he climbed to his feet and he and Doyle were hustled up the stairs to a first floor room. The curtains were closed and a third gunman stood over a line of hostages seated against a wall. Bodie and Doyle were pushed to the ground.

"English?" asked the hostage next to Bodie after some minutes.

Bodie nodded.

"You must understand the position.

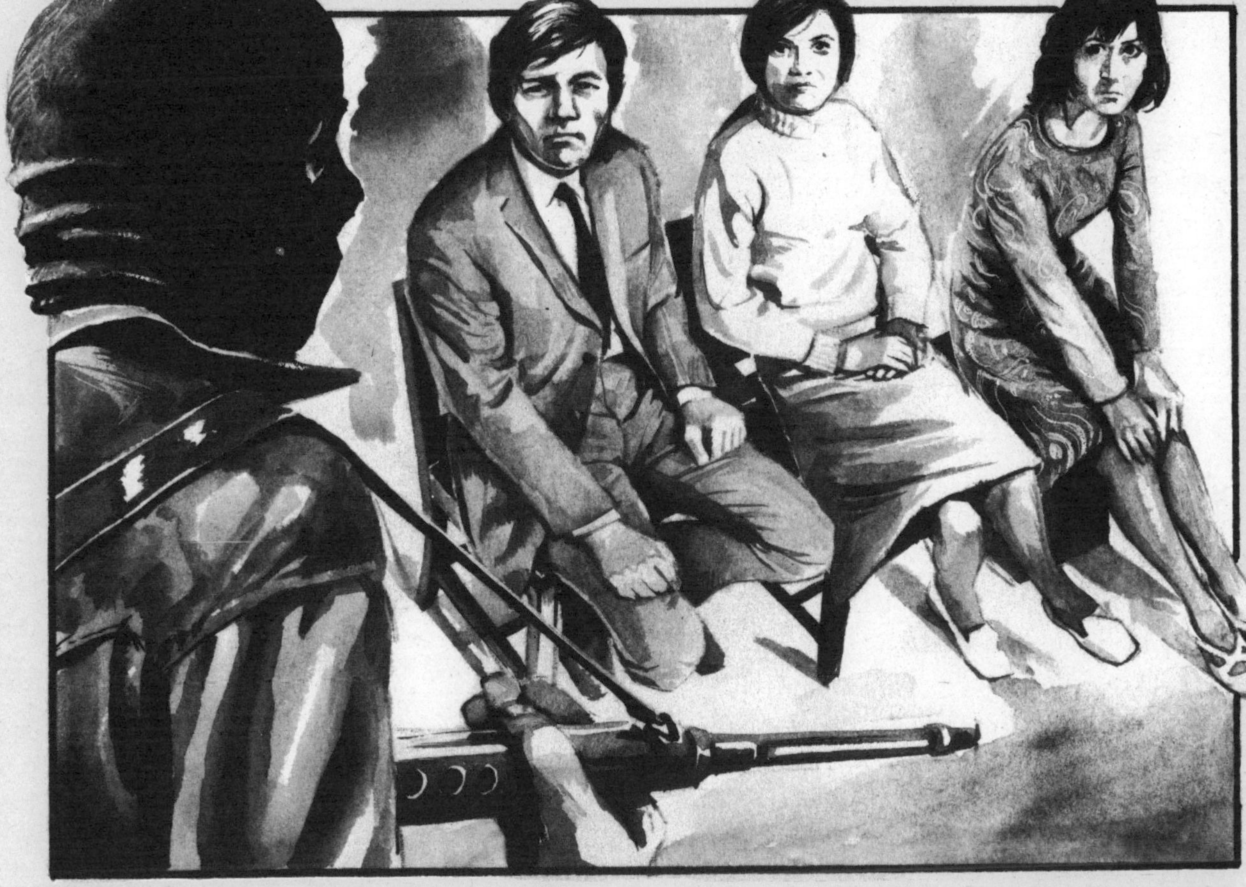

We are all prisoners of these extremists. They hope to engineer the downfall of General Faisak and the destruction of our country."

"What are their demands?"

"The release of all prisoners and the resignation of the government. Of course, General Faisak will not accept these demands."

"And what happens when he refuses?"

"Then we shall be killed," said the man in the same matter of fact tone. "But it will be an honour to die for Faisak, saviour of our people."

"Listen," said Bodie in a low, fierce whisper, "I don't intend dying for anyone just yet; not for Faisak, not for you, not even for your fat uncle Freddie. So tell us how many terrorists there are and just how they intend to blow the place up."

The man looked sullen and averted his gaze. Bodie grasped the man's arm and twisted until he began to talk. "There are three terrorists here. They brought that suitcase you see on the table, the one with the key in it. Inside is a bomb big enough to destroy the building. All it needs to detonate it is for someone to turn the key."

Bodie fingered the fake grenade he had taped to the small of his back. The terrorists had missed it. "Maybe we could bluff them with our grenades," he whispered.

Doyle shook his head. "These guys are too desperate, they don't care if they die. And I wouldn't count on any help from any of our fellow hostages either. They're under the impression that getting blown to bits for the great and glorious Faisak will make them heroes and martyrs."

"Someone should tell them about dead heroes," muttered Bodie.

Suddenly and eerily the sound of Cowley's voice, amplified and distorted by a loudhailer, drifted up to the curtained window from somewhere in the street below. He was asking the terrorists to negotiate.

One of the two hooded men crossed to the window, peered round the curtains and smashed one of the windowpanes with the Kalashnikov's barrel. "Our demands are already known. None of them are negotiable."

"Then release some of your hostages. Give us some assurance that you do not intend people to die needlessly."

"No hostages can be released until our demands are met."

"Then we shall talk again in an hour," said Cowley's voice.

Bodie turned worriedly to Doyle. "He doesn't know it's for real. He thinks that we're still calling the shots."

"I know. And these guys are working on short fuse."

"We've got to make our move soon. There are only three of them and one is permanently downstairs in the hall. Now when Cowley calls from the street one of the remaining two is going to go over to the window to talk to him. That leaves just the one guarding us. We won't get a better opportunity. If we can get hold of one of those rifles then at least we stand a chance."

A tense hour passed in which the three gunmen argued fiercely with one another in Arabic and spat insults at their hostages. Then once more Cowley's voice came up from the street. "Can you hear me? Release some hostages and we can begin negotiations."

Once again one of the gunmen crossed to the window and replied. However this time it was with an angry, incomprehensible shout and a burst of fire. Bodie and Doyle heard sudden, startled screaming from outside the window and knew it was time to act. Doyle dived head first at the man standing before them while

Bodie endeavoured to knock the rifle barrel aside. He did so just as the guard fired, the bullets spattering into the plaster above the hostages' heads and leaving a scar across the wall and through a portrait of General Faisak. "The window, Bodie," yelled Doyle as his partner grabbed the Kalashnikov from the prostrate gunman. Bodie squeezed the trigger as he fell and the second gunman was spun round with the impact of the bullets, shattering what remained of the glass as he fell through the window onto the balcony. Bodie turned to see Doyle knocking the prone gunman unconscious with a rabbit punch. Behind him the third gunman appeared in the doorway. Bodie fired once more and the man crumpled up against the wall, the unfired Kalashnikov cradled in his lap. Doyle was already dragging the hostages to their feet. "All right. Down the stairs and out of the front door as quickly as you can," he yelled.

Outside Cowley had guessed that something was wrong after the first burst of automatic fire. Consequently, as soon as the hostages emerged into the daylight he was prepared and he and his men rushed them across the street to the safety of a protective cordon of cars. Bodie and Doyle were the last to leave the building, both grinning with obvious relief at how lucky they had been. "Are you all right?" Cowley called from across the street.

"Sure," called back Bodie. "There are three gunmen in there. Two of them are dead and the other's unconscious." But even as he spoke there was a tremendous explosion and the two men were lifted bodily into the air and then flung to the ground in a blizzard of flying glass and bricks. Behind them, in a roaring chaos of smoke and flame, melting metal and fragmenting stone, the Embassy had ceased to exist.

When Bodie awoke he was in a hospital bed. At its foot stood Doyle and Cowley. His head ached and reaching up he found it wrapped in bandages.

"What happened?" he asked.

"Just concussion. You should be out in a couple of days."

"But they blew up the Embassy?"

"Either the guy I hit wasn't unconscious or the other guy wasn't quite dead. One of them got to the suitcase and turned the key. Then Boom. Up goes the Embassy."

"Rashid?"

Doyle looked at Cowley and Cowley looked at his feet.

"Rashid's dead," said Doyle.

"He was still in the Embassy when it went up?" asked Bodie.

"He was dead before that," said Cowley. "You shot him."

Bodie's head began to ache. He rubbed his brow with his fingertips as Cowley explained.

"Intelligence got it wrong. Rashid had disappeared to set up a raid on the Embassy. He'd been in touch with other exiles and they'd asked him to do something to draw the world's attention to Faisak's regime."

"So he set up a siege," said Doyle. "Not very original for a professor."

"But I thought —" began Bodie.

"Don't worry," Cowley cut in, "it's not your fault these people chose London to settle their differences."

But the pain in Bodie's head wouldn't go away.

"We're sent to rescue someone and I killed him," he said quietly. "Faisak couldn't have planned it better himself."

"Rashid got what he wanted," said Cowley, "the story's all over the papers. You saved innocent people from getting killed. As for Faisak . . ." Cowley's cheeks twitched as he gazed out of the hospital window. "...We'll just have to wait . . ."

STUNT MAN IN ACTION

Photos by Chris Davies

Most of the time, the stuntman is the elusive mystery man who flashes across your screen in the middle of a piece of exciting action and if you catch a glimpse of him at all, he looks remarkably like the actor whose place he has taken.

His job is to step in and use his expertise to make you think that the dangerous stunt he is doing is being done by someone else!

In "The Professionals" series, Lewis Collins and Martin Shaw do most of their own stunts but there comes a time for the real stuntman to step in.

Very often, of course, the stuntman is not taking the place of the hero but of the villain. In this sequence of film, shot especially for "The Professionals" Annual, stuntman, Mark Boyle, actually played the role of the villain and temporarily became an actor too!

It was an episode called "Kickback" and Mark played a villain who was trying to evade a helicopter pursuit by Bodie. Unfortunately for the villain, his car met up with a tractor in a narrow country lane.

Here's a step by step record of how they set up the crash and made the car roll over

Prop man Barry Arnold adds a little padding to the anti-roll bars which are fixed to form a protective shell around the car's interior.

Mark Boyle has a hole punched through the smashed windscreen and adds a final touch.

Mark Boyle's 50 mph crash up the ramp, shatters the windscreen.

A deathly hush on the unit as the car lands, inverted and wrecked but bang on target and in camera.

The car rolls onto its roof.

It's difficult to imagine anyone emerging but, without a bruise, Mark Boyle squeezes out of the passenger window to a round of applause from the unit.

Director, Ian Sharp, gives Mark a grateful hug.

TEST OF STRENGTH

A large black swastika hung at the back of the dusty shop window. In front of it, surrounded by bayonets and S.S. medals, beneath a sign which said WARTIME CURIOS in bold red lettering, stood a tailor's dummy, dressed in the uniform of a Gestapo colonel, with its arm held high in a Nazi salute, and its bright blue eyes staring sightlessly into the busy street. Had they been able, the dummy's glass eyes would have seen the unsavoury spectacle of the large fat man sweating copiously as he waited on the pavement outside the shop, his fingers drumming impatiently on his brief case until a taxi arrived. Had they been exceptionally keen, the eyes might have noticed the camera, raised and trained on this same man, peeping briefly from the window of an unmarked CI5 car parked some way down the street.

"His name's Nettledorf," said Cowley, the following morning, flipping the photographs across his desk to Doyle and Bodie. "Wealthy, single... little background of interest to us. The shop is an information station."

"Who for?"

"Have you ever heard of the Union of Strength?"

"Sure," said Doyle. "They're an international organisation dedicated to the return of Nazism and the Thousand Year Reich. They're pretty big in some countries but here they're strictly Mickey Mouse — a chewing gum operation full of dodgy looking headbangers and crackpot bigots."

"Save the character reference Doyle, this is serious."

"Come on chief, these thugs have no political clout over here."

"Maybe not. But they have a worldwide set-up remember, and some of their members know all about the workings of power. And something is definitely cooking. Take a look at this report from intelligence."

Bodie took the report and began to study it. It concerned the death of Luke Stevens, a mineral surveyor for a large multi national consortium, who had recently returned from working in a tiny Central American state. According to the report Stevens had last been seen alive hailing a taxi at Heathrow outside the arrivals building. Three days later he had been found shot to death beneath one of the piers of the East India Dock.

"Where's the connection?"

"Bear with me. The taxi was a set up.

We checked all the legit operators out of there. None of them took him. He was as good as dead as soon as he got in."

"Fare's come no higher," murmured Doyle looking down at the photograph of Stevens. "What was he doing in Central America?"

"Surveying for a multi national looking for new investments. The mountains where he was working are part of a very poor country; as poor and corrupt as a banana republic can get. Generalissimo Garcia runs the place with the help of mercenaries and black market guns."

"I know the kind of place," said Doyle, "the rich ride round in their Mercedes while in the barrios the poor scratch round in the dirt with their hens."

Cowley ignored the interruption. "One day Stevens turns up at our consulate and refuses to leave. Word has it he was very frightened and claimed there had been unknown parties making attempts on his life. Eventually, with his beard and moustache shaved off and a new suit of clothes donated by the consular officials he was persuaded to leave and take the plane home. Even then he was careful and took a roundabout route home through Trinidad, Panama, and Jamaica. He carried no luggage, only a briefcase that contained his survey papers and travel documents. When he was found there was no case."

"But our neo Nazi friend here has a briefcase," said Bodie, looking down at the photograph of Nettledorf.

"And granny bonds to old buttons says it's the same one. Another thing: ballistics recovered some fragments from the bullets that killed him. They came from an old German army luger. That brings it back to Nettledorf or one of his friends again."

"You want him brought in?"

"Not yet. Nettledorf has names. With them we can close down the Union of Strength for keeps. Anyway,

there's more to the puzzle. You remember Vine and de Witt."

Bodie grimaced. "Murder and armed robbery. We put them away three years ago. Doyle still has the scars on his arm to remind him."

"The Union of Strength plans to spring them tomorrow night."

Bodie looked incredulous. Doyle said, "that doesn't make sense. What would a bunch of weird political extremists want with a couple of bad boys?"

"That's what we have to find out. All the messages between the two prisoners and the Union have been smuggled in or out. They've never met face to face. That means we can add our own little twist to the situation. The Vine and de Witt that they spring won't be Vine and de Witt."

Bodie knew the answer but he asked anyway: "then who's going over the wall tomorrow night?"

Cowley smiled without humour. "You two," he said.

* * * * * * * * *

There was a muffled explosion from the windows and a padded metal cannister whistled through the bars of the window from which earlier Bodie and Doyle had removed the pane of glass. The cannister struck the ceiling and then the far wall, trailing a length of nylon rope behind it. "Our invitation to the party," said Doyle, reaching down beneath the bunk to retrieve the cannister and unscrewing its lid. "Right on time." From inside he handed a hacksaw blade to Bodie and removed a second for himself.

Five minutes later the bars were gone and the nylon rope stretched out taught into the darkness. Bodie and Doyle were both wearing harnesses they had taken from the cannister and to each harness was attached a hook and pulley. "Here goes," said Bodie attaching his pulley to the rope. Then he stepped from the ledge, one hundred and fifty feet up in the air. Doyle watched him slip away into the night and then, when the darkness had swallowed him, watched the rope from which his friend's life hung suspended dance and vibrate against the stumps of the prison bars. Suddenly it stopped and a light flashed briefly. Now it was his turn. He made sure the harness was fast around his waist, hooked the pulley to the rope and stepped out. The night air was cold around him. The only sound was the creak of the pulley as it ran along the rope. Slowly he gathered momentum.

He knew what to expect and when the dark bulk of the prison wall loomed from the darkness he met it with his outstretched legs. In an instant he had scrambled on top of it and was leaping down the far side, leaping down through a large rectangular hole cut into the roof of a furniture van that stood with its engine idling. His fall was cushioned by sacks of polystyrene granules but before he could regain his balance and find his feet the van was moving. Suddenly he felt a pistol barrel pressed against the nape of his neck. "Welcome to the Union of Strength, Mister de Witt," said a voice behind him.

* * * * * * * * *

It was in the early light of morning that the van crunched up in the gravel drive to a large country house. Peacocks slept beneath the trees and traces of morning mist drifted across the lawns. Two armed guards ushered Bodie and Doyle from the back of the van and into the house. There two more guards stood either side of them. A suit of armour stood at the foot of the stairs and half way up, where it turned, was draped a large red flag emblazoned with a black swastika. "These guys are from the B pictures," Doyle muttered to his partner, "they couldn't take over a pancake factory, let alone a country. Look at their artillery. It's so old it's dangerous. Lugers and Schmeissers. Even a Jap Hanbu. They were dangerous even when they were new and that was forty years ago. Now I wouldn't like to be either end of one if it went off. You wouldn't be safe either end. I tell you these guys are crazy."

"That's why they're dangerous," hissed back Bodie as a guard prodded him in the back with a Mauser sub machine gun, propelling the two men down a series of corridors to a set of double doors. In the room beyond

them, behind a mahogany desk and in front of a portrait of Adolf Hitler, sat Nettledorf. "Welcome, gentlemen," smiled the fat man, "You are now in the presence of one of the world's future leaders. I ask you: don't you feel a certain humility at being invited to advance our grand design?"

"How do you expect us to do that?"

"By the practice of your trade, Mr. Vine. By stealing money."

"How much money?"

"Approximately four million pounds. The Union of Strength expect you to carry out a series of bank and bullion robberies for them. Once these are completed you will be smuggled from the country and be free men once more."

"And if we refuse?"

"You will wish you had stayed in prison."

"I told you they were all crazy," whispered Doyle.

"Can we have time to talk about it?"

"Certainly. You have five minutes."

They were marched down a series of corridors and locked in a bare room. Bodie heard a single guard pacing up and down outside. Both men were tense and ready.

"We know what they want from us. We still don't know why."

"And we've three minutes left to find out. You remember the route back to Feuhrer Nettledorf?"

Bodie nodded.

"Then let's call the guard."

Bodie and Doyle were professionals. They had been trained by CI5. The guard had not and the outcome to the struggle was never in doubt.

"Okay," said Doyle, leaning over the unconscious guard and gingerly removing the Hanbu pistol from his belt, "let's get going."

The two men ran in a low crouch down the twisting maze of corridors. Bodie hit the double doors first, bursting them open with his shoulder and knocking the guard who stood behind them to his knees. Doyle came in after him, vaulting the desk and planting two flying feet in the centre of Nettledorf's chest. The chair tilted backward and the Nazi was flung to the floor. Doyle pressed the Hanbu to his head as more guards appeared in different doorways to the room. "Hold it where you are or I send one of the world's future leaders straight down the tubes."

"He means it boys, he's a fanatic when it comes to politics," said Bodie laconically as he retrieved the sub machine gun from the spreadeagled guard.

"Do as they say, men," said Nettledorf, "we have nothing to fear from these ruffians. The Union can buy and sell men of ten times their mettle."

"Right now you've no takers," said Bodie and gestured with the machine gun. "Drop your weapons and get in there." He indicated an open door. "Nettledorf, call the rest of your men."

It went without a hitch. Doyle kept the pistol pointed at Nettledorf's head

and as each of the guards entered Bodie disarmed them and ushered them into the side room with their comrades. "Are there any more?" asked Bodie after the nineteenth.

The fat man shook his head and Bodie locked the door.

"All right, Nettledorf, get your papers together, we're going for a ride. And don't forget Stevens' briefcase."

Suspicion replaced fear in Nettledorf's face as Doyle dragged him roughly to his feet. "What do you know about Stevens?" he asked.

"Only that you had him killed."

"It was a necessary murder. He became a sacrifice to our glorious purpose. But I see such ideas as honour, duty, and sacrifice are alien to the mentality of two common criminals."

"Should we tell him?" asked Bodie.

Doyle shook his head. "Leave that to Cowley." Then he looked at the ancient Japanese gun in his hand, and said to his friend, "I'll tell you something, Bodie." Bodie looked at him. "I'm glad I didn't have to fire this damn thing."

Cowley looked across his desk at Bodie and Doyle. He was pleased with his two men but knew better than to say so. "Thanks to those papers you brought in we've managed to clean up the Union of Strength in five European countries."

"Did you find out why they shot Stevens?"

"For his survey reports. It turns out that the mountains Stevens surveyed contain some of the richest mineral deposits in the Western world. The Union of Strength realised what political power that could give them and they wanted in. In fleabag dictatorships the fastest way in is with bribes."

"So they wanted to spring de Witt and Vine to steal them the bribe money."

"They wanted to buy half the country and a man like the Generalissimo would have been only too willing to sell, especially as the Union of Strength would have guaranteed his security . . . so long as he was still useful to them."

"You think they could have pulled it off?" asked Bodie.

"I don't know," said Cowley, shaking his head, "these people might seem like cranks, but put them together and they're a different proposition. If they'd been able to buy their way in from the off . . . who knows? Anyway, our American colleagues inform me that the Generalissimo's days as the great dictator are now distinctly numbered."

"So all will be freedom and light over there?"

Cowley buzzed for his secretary.

"Don't be facetious, Doyle," he said crisply. "There will be another government there, another set of leaders. Let's just hope they are people we can deal with."

REMEMBER THESE?